AF556464

Environment Degradation and Rural Poverty

ENVIRONMENT DEGRADATION AND RURAL POVERTY

By

M. Soundarapandian
Reader
Department of Rural Industries and Management,
Gandhigram Rural Institute, Deemed University
Gandhigram–624 302

DISCOVERY PUBLISHING HOUSE
NEW DELHI

First Published–2005

ISBN: 81-8356-014-8

Published by:

DISCOVERY PUBLISHING HOUSE

4831/24, Prahlad Street, Ansari Road, Darya Ganj
New Delhi–110 002 (India)
Phone: 23279245, • Fax: 91-11-23253475
e-mail: dphtemp@indiatimes.com

Printed at: Amit Enterprises, Delhi

Preface

The revolution in science and technology, growth of population and intensive industrial development have brought about the environmental crisis in India. There is also relation between the environment degradation and income of the people. The environment protection will lead to the economic development by way of income and employment generation in the agricultural sector. The study aims to analyse the impact of environment degradation on the level of living of the farmers in rural areas. The findings of the study would provide guidelines for the policy decisions on the environment protection and alleviation of the rural poverty.

I am thankful to the University Grants Commission, New Delhi, for providing the financial assistance for undertaking the vital issue as major research project for the period of two years. I am grateful to Dr. G. Pankajam, Vice-Chancellor, and the authorities of the Gandhigram Rural Institute for providing the facilities to undertake the study in this institute.

My profound thanks to Dr. N. Thillainayagam, Professor and Head, Department of Rural Industries and Management, Gandhigram Rural Institute for his encouragement to complete the work within the stipulated period. It gives me a pleasure to thank Dr. C. Rajkumar, Research Fellow of this project, my wife Mrs. S. Indumathi and my children S. Diwakaran and S. Vidya for their cooperation in completing the project work.

M. Soundarapandian

Contents

1

INTRODUCTION

STATEMENT OF THE PROBLEM

Environment problems center on human activities which can adversely affect the atmosphere, oceans and land cover global, national and local concerns, ranging from global warming and ozone depletion, to depreciation and soil erosion, contamination of fresh water resources and urban pollution. Many developing countries are concerned about issues such as soil erosion, water pollution, urban air pollution and desertification, which impinge on the relationship between poverty and environmental degradation. Rapid population growth places enormous pressure on all aspects of the environment and combined with deforestation, land degradation and soil erosion, which is causing increase in the numbers of these living in extreme poverty.

Almost half of India's arable land, 150 million hectares, has become barren due to indiscriminate use of chemicals and complete removal of biomass after harvesting. It takes nearly 500 years to build an inch of top soil. With modern agricultural practices, according to one estimate, a farm loss one-inch of top soils every 16 years. M.S. Swaminathan had warned in 1968 that indiscriminate and unscientific use of chemical methods could lead to agricultural disasters instead of prosperity.

According to Dinamalar (Daily) data lab, (3.10.1997), of the average rainfall of 400 millions hectare metre in India, 225 million hectare metre go into the groundwater potentials. The industrial waste pollutes the groundwater potentials.

Without proper maintenance of effluent plant for industrial waste from leather, paper, textile and chemical based industries; environmental degradation has been developed in India.

Government of India listed out the 2000 industries, which create environmental pollution in India. Of the total 2000 industries (nearly 50 per cent industries) are located in Tamil Nadu. In Tamil Nadu, 655 industries are distributing the wastewater directly into the rives. The content of the industrial waste water like chromium, mercury and organic, affects the health of ocean animals.

According to the Land Use Statistics(LUS), the total extent of lands that suffer from degradation, to a greater or less degree, is 175 M.he. Since this figure obviously includes wastelands, it follows that the country possesses, around 150 M.he. suffer from erosion of the topsoil and its attendant ills (such as floods and gully formation, etc.) are around 25 M.he. from water logging and salinisation. Of the lands subject to erosion, around 125 M.he. suffer from water erosion and around 25 M.he from wind erosion.

According to the National Commission for Agriculture (NCA), about 6. M.ha. of agricultural land suffer from water logging and 7M.ha. from soil salinity and alkalinity. The present study attempts to analyse the environmental degradation and its impact on the poor people in a backward region of Tamil Nadu.

OBJECTIVES OF THE STUDY

The specific objectives of the study are:

1. To study the impact of land degradation at macro level on net area sown and yield rate of major crops during 1985-86 to 1994-95 in Tamil Nadu;

2. To find out the relation between land and water resources degradation and the occupational structure, employment and income level of the farmers in the South Tamil Nadu area; and

3. To suggest the proper land and water resource management policies to enhance the income of the farmers in the study area.

CONCEPTS

The following concepts were used in the present study.

Drought Prone Area

Drought prone area is generally identified on the low extent of irrigated area, low erratic distribution of rainfall and high periodically of drought.

Small Farmers

A cultivator with a land holding of 5 acres or below is a small farmer. In the case of irrigated land as defined in the State Land Ceiling legislation, a farmer with 2.5 acre or less will also be considered as a small farmer where the land is irrigated but not of the class 1 variety.

Marginal Farmers

A person with a land holding of 2.5 acres or below is a marginal farmer. In the case of class I irrigated land, the ceiling will be one acre.

Large Farmers

A person with a land holding 5.0 acres or above is a large farmer.

Agricultural Labourers

A person without any land, but with a homestead and deriving more than 50 per cent of his income from agricultural wages is an agricultural labour.

Non-Agricultural Labourers

Persons, who derive their income partly from agriculture and partly from other sources can also be brought under this category, provided at least 50 per cent of their income is from non-agricultural sources. They need not have a homestead but must be residents of the village in which they are identified.

Arid Areas

Areas with rainfall upto 375 mm per year are considered as Arid Areas.

Semi-Arid Areas

Areas with rainfall from 375 mm to 750 mm per year are also considered as semi Arid Areas.

Cropping Pattern

It is defined as the percentage of area different crops to the total cropped area of the farm at a point of time. Cropping pattern is computed by using following formula.

$$\text{Cropping pattern of ith crop} = \frac{\text{Area Cultivated for ith crop}}{\text{Total Area Cultivated for all crop}} \times 100$$

Poverty

Poverty broadly refers to lack of means to satisfy a person basic needs and other essential of life. Such needs may be defined narrowly as those necessary for survival or more broadly as determined by the prevailing standard of living in the community. Poverty is caused by lack of assets combined with low and uncertain returns to the limited stock of assets owned by the farmers. Poverty includes access to service, wages and prices, unemployment and educational etc.

Environmental Degradation

The environmental degradation is wearing down of land, rocks, or other land formation, by erosion. The degrading of complex chemical components on the surrounding things, conditions, and inherence, affecting the growth of living things differences in environment often account for differences in plants of the same kind found in different places and the conditions of the air, water, soil, plants, animals and natural.

Soil Erosion

Soil erosion is often related to decline in soil quality, caused through its misuse by humans. It refers to a decline in the soil productivity through adverse changes in nutrient status and soil organic matter, structural attributes, and concentration of electrolytes and toxic chemicals.

Water Erosion

Water erosion is that takes place in land slides and floods, while cutting trees for firewood, agricultural implements and timber, grazing by large capacity of grass land traditional agricultural practices, construction of roads, indiscriminate (lime stone) quarrying and other activities, have all led to the opening of hill faces to deserts dusts, storms, whirlwinds and destruction of crops, while moving sand covers the land and makes it sterile.

METHODOLOGY—DESIGN OF THE STUDY

The present study used primary as well as secondary data. Secondary data were used to analyse the regional level environmental degradation over a period of 10 years from 1985-86 to 1994-95. Census data, data from agricultural department, topo-sheets of survey of India were analysed cartographically, graphically and statistically to arrive at conclusion. Later, present land use pattern was compared with the previous land use pattern and occupational planning for backward region.

Virudhunagar, Tirunelveli and Tuticorin Districts are purposively selected for the study because the researcher is familiar with the Districts. One sample Block was selected from each district on the basis of the large number of farmers. After selecting the sample block for the study, one village panchayat in the block was selected on the basis of the same criteria.

Three districts were selected in the study region. The study districts are (i) Virudhu Nagar District-hilly and plain areas without perennial river; (ii) Tirunelveli district-Tamirabarani river and hilly areas; and (iii) V.O. Chidambaranar district (Now Tuticorin district). Industrially developed and coastal areas. Through multistage sampling method, three villages were selected as representative villages from each district.

Virudhungar district is a drought prone district and there is no perennial river in the district. The agricultural lands fully depend on the rainfall and ground water resources. The cotton textile mills, cement industry and small scale cottage industries like match industry, printing, fireworks are concentrated in this district.

Tirunelveli district is the agricultural district with a river Thamirabarani. One highly developed cement industry, few textile mills, match industry, and beedi industry have been developed in this district.

Tuticorin district is an coastal district. It has the main industry like Spic, TAG, Sterlite which affect, the environment gradually and ports and power plants are also concentrated in this district. So, these three districts having distinguishing character have been selected for the present study.

In order to analyse the relationship between the changes in land and the changes water resources and occupational structure, employment and income pattern of the farmers, primary data were collected.

A sample of 150 farmers (Small, Marginal, Large) from the three sample villages (one village panchayat from each district) were randomly selected with the help of verifying land holdings. A total of 450 farmers were randomly selected and administered with a pretested questionnaire. The collected data were analysed with suitable statistical tools.

The primary data on various aspects were collected during the year 2000-2001. Discussions were made with the farmers in order to identify the reasons for the land degradations and made comparison between the years 1993-94 and 2000-2001 in South Tamil Nadu.

The respondent's response to each of the question in the schedule was first tabulated in master table. The qualitative data were quantified as discussed and tabulated to drawn meaningful inferences. There after, appropriate tables were prepared keeping in view the specific objectives of the study for analysing the data with the application of statistical tools. Simple average and tabular analysis was used to analyse of the data. Before (1993-94) and after (2000-2001) technique and comparative analysis were also used to study the Environmental Degradation and Poverty in Backward Region of South Tamil Nadu.

IMPORTANCE OF THE STUDY

The revolution in science and technology and the intensive industrial development along with excessive utilization of resources has brought about global environment crisis the most alarming of the environmental problems in the mans assaults upon the environment by contaminating the air, earth and water of the surroundings region, which ultimately results in the degradation of environment quality. Geographic contribution in environmental studies are very useful as it investigate carefully environmental problems in relation to input, yield, employment, income and also analyse the environmental quality.

Agricultural economists in India have so far shown more interest in the economics of crop production rather than in the environmental economy. There has been some exploration of the inter-relationship between agricultural growth and rural poverty. But the impact of agricultural development on rural ecology and poverty has attracted very little attention.

In view of rapid population growth and shortages of food grains, fibres and oil seeds, it is understandable that the attention of the policy makers and the academics alike should be focused mainly on the crop economy. Like wise, the over riding need to achieve self sufficiency in a sensitive sectors like food grains and it has served to attract the attention from an equally important question of raising the level of the poor. Further more, the preoccupation with the challenges in the crop production sector have made the planners, until recently, for growing ecological imbalances caused by a particular pattern of agricultural development pursued in the country.

The persistence of rural poverty despite the attainment of self-sufficiency in food grains has generated interest in the pursuit of strategies and programmes for the alleviation of poverty. Moreover the extensive deforestation and ecological degradation resulting in the loss of water table and shortages of fuel wood and fodder have brought to the issue of long run sustainability of agricultural growth itself apart from the question of protecting and improving the livelihood of the rural poor through environmental conservation.

Although economists have not given attention to the analysis of the impact of environmental degradation on agricultural development through irrigation to eradicate poverty, there is a need to understand the causes of technological changes in the irrigation vis-à-vis rural poverty. The findings of the study will be useful to the planners and policy makers to reduce the environment degradation and poverty level with the development of the farm sector in backward region of Tamil Nadu.

REVIEW OF LITERATURE

The present chapter reviews past studies related to environment degradation and poverty and it is classified into three sections. First section explains the studies on environment degradation, the second section deals with the studies on poverty and the third section presents the studies on environmental degradation and poverty.

Environmental Degradation

Jose Jacob[1] study revealed that large scale irrigation projects are not only suitable for the agricultural development on account of the state's topographical peculiarities and ecological implications, but also misfit in the economic where withdrawal of the state. Evolving of a model of irrigation system that does fit in the economic limits of the state and at the same time herewith the requirements of the state is one of the matters of core significance. For the reason of irrigating crop other than paddy being more productive and economically viable, development of small and tiny irrigation scheme appear to offer a better solutions to the irrigation needs of the state.

Attar Sing[2] conducted a study on the impact of floods on various aspects of land use, cropping characteristics and the environmental degradation problems in the selected areas. The study highlighted the problems of flood prone areas in a semi-arid river-basin zone and points out that the impact of flood affects the living conditions of the people The study reveals that nearly 58 per cent of the total geographical area of Bharatpur district is flood intensity prone, of which a major portion is found in the low flood intensity zone. High flood intensity is found in a very limited area.

Over the past three years, nearly 95 per cent of land in the village of Madhya Pradesh has been bundled to prevent soil erosion. Farm ponds have been built to store water for a second crop. The underground dyes have been built to raise the water level in nearby wells. Experiments have been conducted to raise agricultural yields and control use of chemical fertilizers and pesticides. And on the environment side, soil erosion appears to have largely ended, water tables seen to have risen and there is more greedy around than three years ago[3].

The review of Sankaram Ayala,[4] that the regional difference in productivity must disappears. The best hope lies in the adoption of eco-technologies with vigour and veracity over the next decade. The problem is one of assembling and distribution of the resources in the rural areas for green manure seeds, compost, silt from tanks and irrigation channels, bio-pesticides, utilization of solar and wind energy in chose areas. Indian farmers must be trained to forget the past with no regret. The future with ecotechnologies is assumed for economic yield maximization, resurgence of the soil and environmental health for stability and unsustainability.

Murugan *et al.*[5] revealed that this modern crop production technology has considerably raised output but has created problems of land degradation. Pesticide residues in farm produce, gene erosion, atmospheric and water pollution. The natural resources base has degraded and diminished and the quality of environmental sustaining human life has adversely been affected. With the increase in population from 560 million in 1951 to about 987 million by this century. Our compulsion will be not only to agriculture production but also increase it further in a sustainable way through organic farming. Under limited supply of organic resources, our target can be achieved by blending modern technology in harmony with traditional technology. Sustainable agriculture should involve successful management of resources to satisfy the quality of the environment and conserving natural resources.

Ganesamoorthy[6] expressed that the technical facilities must be constantly on land to collect and process data and disseminate the knowledge gained appropriately. The accelerating decline in land and soil quality and the slow progress made in promoting more sustainable management methods would justify the nature reserves, natural heritage sites which would help to protect plants and animals in their natural habitats. Such an arrangement would also facilitate the co-ordination of regional environmental strategies. New programmes could place greater emphasis on the management of soil and water resources.

Intensive cultivation of land without conservation of soil fertility and soil structure leads ultimately to the springing up of deserts, irrigation without arrangements for drainage resulted in soil setting alkaline or saline. Indiscriminate use of pesticides, fungicides and herbicides could cause adverse changes in biological balance as well as lead to an increase in the incidence of cancer and other disease through the toxic residues present in the grains or other edible parts. Unscientific tapping of underground water leads to the rapid expansion of the capital resources. The main suggestions of the study are: Appropriate institutional structures to be formulated to organise farmers for collective action, legal structures to manage groundwater through appropriate local organisation etc.[7]

Muthukumar and Rajendren[8] made a study on the functional aspects of voluntary organisation engaged in development work. The study was carried out to understand the role of a voluntary organisation Alternative for Indian

Development(AID), in bringing about sustainability in the areas of water resources. The study highlighted the central issues of raising voluntary action for sustainable development in general and water resources in particular.

Rajeev *et al.*[9] analysed the crop sequence with short duration rice cultivated in kuruvai followed by ratoon rice. The results clearly emphasise the added advantage of inclusion of ratoon rice in the cropping sequence, which resulted in high cropping intensity and more gross and net income and return per rupee invested. Thus, crop sequence with ratoon rice is cost effective, cheap and an effective toll to achieve the desired goal of sustainable agriculture in flood prone areas.

Chinniah and *et al.*[10] classified the human impacts upon groundwater system in three ways i.e.

1. Direct use of groundwater for water supply industry or irrigation and the problems associated with it.
2. Impact due to hydraulic schemes of surface waters upon the groundwater and groundwater contamination due to numerous other activities.
3. And the study revealed that the source of future irrigation in groundwater development may involved by increasing trend of groundwater and heavy extraction may induce seawater intrusion in the coastal areas.

Karthikeyan *et al.*[11] suggested that when the rural domestic energy is improved the research on food chain structure of ecosystem should be emphasised to increase the stability of the system. The living things in the system depend on and inhibit each other. The flow and conversion of energy materials depend on the food chain net. Therefore, the food chain structure should be gradually set up to promote multiple utilization of bio-mass with no or minimal wastes. In doing so, the ecosystem can be favourably developed and the environment can be greatly developed in our nation.

Jitendra Kumar Sinha[12] revealed that draught is a natural hazard generally caused by deficient rainfall and overuse of groundwater. To mitigate its effects a suitable mix of policy reform and, institutional changes are needed. Storage of water, rainwater harvesting, watershed approach to rainfed farming and development of drought resistant crop varieties are some steps to effectively check the impact of drought.

Navin Chandra Johsi[13] said that the Government has embarked upon a massive programme of waste lands development. So that these lands become green and fertile within the shortest possible time. It has been found that watershed technology and programmes can be used for improving the use of land and water resources. Wherever they were implemented, they have proved highly cost-effective and a great help in increasing the moisture content of the soil, thereby preventing soil erosion, leading to increase in bio-mass and reclamation of wastelands.

Dhulasi Brirundha[14] pointed out that environment management is now directed at matching environmental policy to the socio-economic goals. Specially, environment management policy has to define how without grossly compromising other equally relevant but often competing or conflicting socio aspirations for improved quality of life. enhanced development opportunity, equitable income distribution, availability of needed energy, gainful employment and leisure time activities. Thus environmental management as currently projected, is a comprehensive, multiple-goal strategy for environmentally sound resource utilization for attaining the politically desirable socio-economic status for all people, while at the same time conserving vital sectors of the environment.

Gapalakrishnan *et al.*[15] conducted a morphometric study on Kodayar River Basin in Kanyakumari District. The Kodayar River Basin covers an area of about 300 sq kms. The Kodavar river basin is an fifth order basin with a bifurcation ration of 4:4 indicating a mature stage of development. The slope and hyphometric analysis have been carried out for the basin. The hyphometric analysis also indicates the mature stage of development of the basin. From the analysis, it can be inferred that the physiography has major influence over other factors.

Noor Mohammad[16] study is modest attempt to (i) assess the agricultural development (ii) examine the environmental degradation and (iii) find out the correlation between the two in the Sonipat district of Haryana. Firstly on the basis of this secondary data agricultural development has ascertained at block level by taking as many as 13 indicators of different nature and the character "Z" scores have been used to standardize them. Five indicators viz. forest areas and cover soil erosion, water logging salinitv and alkalinity and sinking of water tale have been taken to assess environmental degradation.

The most alarming of the environmental problem is the contamination of air water, land and soil which ultimately results in view, the study provides comprehensive picture of a small area covering various aspects of pollution at different levels. An attempt has been made to find out the over all habitat environmental degradation and quality of life of the Abdullahpur district, Meerut.[17]

The result of the study of Pramanik[18] is that the feeding effect of soil arthropods namely parasol laevis (Isopoda:Crustacean) And Anoplodesmus Saussurel (Polvdesmida Diplopoda) on the rate of leaf litter was compared under microcosm conditions. Commination by both species could enhance release of Calcium and Organic Carbon but efficiency of the diploid was notably more in all the cases. Microbial action on leaf litter was sufficient to realize potassium significantly but in all other cases the detriflovore. Contribution in sequestering nutrients was evident. Feeding interaction between the two species had cumulative and synergistic impact on the enrichment of nutrients in the sand medium. Pesticide of leaf litter through treatment of sublethal concentration of heptacholar 20 Ec, and endosulfan 35 Ec could suppress faunal activity and release of the nutrients. The inhibitory effect of both pesticides could be noticed on the level of calcium and organic carbon. The fauna mediated mobilization or nitrate nitrogen was strongly inhibited by endosulfan whereas that of calcium and potassium over prominently reduced by heptachlor.

Chauhen [19] found that more than 25% of the earth's land surface is threatened by desertification. Over 900 million people in more than 100 countries are at risk. Ninety of these countries are in the developing world. In the past, the problem was seen as a strictly regional one, primarily affecting the dry land areas in parts of Africa, Asia and Latin America. However, studies have shown that land degradation is becoming increasingly widespread.

A study of Emtiazi[20] revels that Aspergillus terreus isolated from rotten wood decolorrise several dyes used in textile industries including Solamin blue, solamine yellow, solamine red, solamine scarlet, Terter direct orange, Terter direct blue and Aniline blue. Decolorisation was favoured when the Aspergillus terrus was grown on wheat straw with cellulose and in peroxides activities. The fungus could biodegrade these dyes and utilize them as the only source of carbon, nitrogen and energy. The COD removal and production of ammonia during biodegradation of dyes by the isolated fungi were investigated.

Desai[21] made a study on changing land use pattern in India Agriculture and pointed out that the utilization of land in India is flexible, even though some types of land uses continuously increased. Conversely some types of land had continuously decreased.

In India, the non-agricultural uses of land during the last a few years increased mainly due to various development activities as well as rapid increase in population. Similarly the permanent pasture and other grazing land also increased. The fallow lands increased due to inadequate supply of water, unremunerative nature of farming, unfavourabe climate etc. Conversely the land under tree crops and grains decreased because there is pressure on land for non-food crops and other raw materials required for industrial development. The current fallow increased generally to restore the fertility of land.

Another study of Sivappan [22] emphasised that in India, 1/3 of the total area is unproductive due to soil erosion and mismanagement of land. Moreover, the percentage of rainfall is very low because of deforestation and mismanagement of water. Presently in India, more than 90% of available water is diverted for agriculture and the proportion will be reduced to 75%-80% in another 10-20 year period. The study suggested the proper land and water management and soil and water conservation practices. More over there is an urgent need for the real conjunctive use of surface and ground water. The rainwater can be harvested in the tank and canal command area of the country.

Isaac Arnon[23] pointed out that ground water development, especially community well irrigation scheme can supplement the supply of surface waters during the dry season. He is very pessimistic about the functioning, quality and administration of Rural Works Programme in the developing countries.

Asok K. Mitra[24] studied on Mula Irrigation Project in Maharashtra, which wa entrused to the Water and Land Management Institute, Aurangabad. The study enquired into the aspects of planning and implementation for fuller and timely development of the irrigation system as well as aspect of management of water distribution and efficient utilization of the potentials created under the system. He discussed pattern of water distribution under canal irrigation and also appraised the functioning of well irrigation.

Yu Xiaogang[25] revealed that free water supplied to urban centers impose costs on the upland watershed. The study analyses the conflicts and costs of such provision of external ecosystem services in a case in Yunnan, China. It argues that in order to internalize the external costs of such water supply, there should be a locally embedded system of forest management. It further argues that pricing of these external ecosystem products, like water, is needed to enable local communities to balance the benefits from their sale against costs and other benefits.

A case study of Wang Qinghna[26] in China brings out the importance of forests in providing various level ecological services that are essential for the system of terraced agriculture. The study investigates local people's knowledge of forest-based ecological services including water regulation and nutrient recycling and gender difference in the local knowledge of these services. The study noted that the Hani have maintained forest condition quite irrespective of its tenurial status.

Padoshri[27] have done a good job by studying the problem in Goa which is not yet intensively studied by individual researchers. The authors stated that Goa's agricultural sector "absorbs more then 70 per cent of the total work force". The inference of the study is about "not so extensive" and found that damage caused to the land is only by the mining industry and their suggestion to undertake an exhaustive study of Goa's forests are articularly noteworthy

A study of Kanachana Chopra[28] examines issue relating to appropriate technology for such management and its sustainability in the context of programmes undertaken by non governmental and non-governmental organisation. The study concluded that the non governmental sectors need to be entrusted for evolving a solution to this pressing problem of land degradation which now affects large areas of the country.

Vaidyanathan[29] study has summarised as progressive lowering of ground water in many parts of the country tends to give rise to concerns about over-exploitations; lowering water table is a genuine warning signal, but in order to judge whether or not there is over exploitation we need to monitor the proportion of dry wells and wells which have gone out of use, the average yield per well, the area irrigated per wells as the conservation measures adopted by the farmers. The government has a crucial role to play in encountering the myopic characteristic of individual and even communities, in the exploitation of deplorable resources like ground water. For this purpose it needs to pay attention to generating more and better information on ground water use in different areas with active involvement of the public and independent experts.

Chandrama Goswami[30] pointed out that the various types of environmental degradation-soil degradation depletion of ground water level, deforestation, soil erosion, floods, water losing, soil salinity, etc., is the negative outcome of the chemical notion of maximizing the economic growth at the cost of the environment. After proper classification of soil and consultation agronomist will indicate what crops can be grown in each district keeping the environmental in view. Productivity of crops have to be increased to feed the increasing population as the limit to extensive cultivation.

Singh[31] found that the Eastern Himalayan region has been blessed by rich natural resources. However, the region has for long suffered from indifference and from insurgency, which has in recent years, become endemic to the region. A healing process could rightly begin, with the government's initiation, and supported by NGOs and the local communities.

Another study of Normen Uphoffeno *et al.*[32] focussed on how the participation of farmers in irrigation management can improve the efficiency, equity and over all performance of irrigation systems in developing countries. A crucial factor in performance has received less in the structure and performance of irrigation agencies that are responsible for managing many or most of these systems in the third World. The author's enthusiasm for performance improvement without major surgery in the design of irrigation organisation is likely to be far from infections.

Dhyani *et al.*[33] argued that adoption of soil and water conservation technologies on farmer's field on watershed basis in the outer Himalayan region is highly economical. Development of irrigation potential coupled with terrace improvement for intensive agriculture and horticulture plantation deserves top priority for the development of hills as they are least lezadory and most rewarding. There is a need to strengthen the use of community land for fodder and pasture development either by continues support of the government or by imposing restriction on the rights of the people on the reserve forest so that they may actively think of utilizing such lands.

Nagaraj *et al.*[34] describes of the well drilling behaviour of farmers in the hand rock areas. With probability of well failure around 0.4, the estimation of total investment in drilling borewells for irrigation purpose is crucial as it provides vital information at micro level for the farmers to set aside sufficient funds for borewell drilling and at macro level for policy makers in earmarking adequate funds for programmes like '100 wells scheme' and Gonga Kalyan Yojana. Such macro irrigation well drilling programmes and other macro level schemes of the Government can properly estimate the total cost of drilling as suggested, instead of just assuming that they would be able to provide a successful well in the very first attempt.

Srinivasamoorthy[35] found out the picture of irrigation investment from the first plan to Seventh plan. He also discusses the share of irrigation investment in total public sector outlay. And he devoted to a discussion of ultimate irrigation potential, plan targets, achievements and crop wise distribution of irrigation water.

In the process, a debate on minor versus major irrigation has emerged. Among the minor irrigation systems the traditionally dominant groundwater irrigation has proved to be more efficient in terms of ensuring higher productivity and intensity of cropping. It is however not totally free from the problems relating to equity, dependability and operational efficiency.[36]

Poverty

Findings showed that the majority of the sample households survived on cereals and had only one main meal per day, as start indicator of food insecurity, female-headed households were the most adversely affected. 'Poverty group' in the study villages irrespective of caste. The landless people's lack of basic needs (clothing, shelter, household equipment, and health care) revealed much more of their better destitution than conventional food intake.[37] Vaidyanathan[38] discusses some important issues concerning concepts and measurement of poverty as well as the design and implementation of policies to tackle the problem.

Danny M. Leipziger[39] compare East Asia, Latin America and the Caribbean in reducing poverty rates, since the 1980's largely because of sluggish growth. Growth should be the core of all country development strategies around which efforts to reduce poverty, broaden citizens participation in government and improved governance can flourish.

Ghosh[40] felt that there is no doubt that combating poverty can not be managed by the government alone. There are many areas where government needs collaboration and cooperation from NGO's particularly in creating opportunity, facilitating empowerment and providing security to the poor. The pressure of the donor agencies on the recipient government to work though NGO's in development programme is also a dominant factor in increasing the role of NGO's to fight against poverty.

The World Development Report[41] in this report recognizes that poverty is more than inadequate income or human development it is also vulnerability and a lack of voice, power and representation. With this multidimensional view, poverty comes greater complexity in poverty reduction strategies, because social and cultural forces need to be taken into account. The way to deal with this complexity is through empowerment and participation-local, national and international. Participatory mechanisms can provide voice to women and men, especially those from poor and excluded segments of society. The design of decentralised agencies and services needs to reflect local conditions. And international institutions should listen to and promote the interests of poor people. The poor are the main actors to fight against poverty. And they must be brought counter stage in designing, implementing, and monitoring antipoverty strategies.

Venkatesh[42] reported that the recent World Development Report deals exclusively with poverty. But it appears that the World Banks has not devoted sufficient thought to the institutions to be setup to carry out poverty alleviation programmes, if one gives by the anti-poverty projects of Andhra Pradesh and Rajasthan, and is repeating the past mistakes.

A study of Deepa Narayan[43] revealed first, that poverty is multidimensional and has important non-economic dimensions; second, that poverty is always specific to a location and a social group, and awareness of these specifics is essential to the design of policies and programs intended to attack poverty; and third, that despite in different places, there are striking in the experience of poverty in very different countries, from Russia to Brazil, Nigeria to Indonesia. Poor people's lives are characterised by powerlessness and voicelessness, which limit their choices and define the quality of their interactions with employees, markets, the state, and even non-governmental organizations (NGOs). Institutions both formal and informal mediate and limit poor people's access to opportunities.

Masood Ahmed and Hugh Bredenkamp[44] reported that the transformation of the Enhanced Structural Adjustment Facility(ESAF) into the Poverty Reduction and Growth Facility(PRGF) has important implications for the design of program supported by the IMF in low-income countries. The emphasis on growth and poverty reduction will directly influence policy choices as well as the pace and sequencing of implementation. The government will take the land in setting the agenda. And the basic buildings blocs of the program—from diagnosis through the design of monitoring indicators– will be subject to broad pubic consultation as a country's poverty reduction strategy is put together. As a result, the specific policy measures supported under a PRFG program will be derived from the country's own poverty reduction strategy.

A country could enjoy a high average growth rate without any benefit to its poorest households if income disparities grew significantly in other words, if the rich got richer while the incomes of the poor stagnated or declined. This outcome is rate, however, income distribution (for example, as measured by the gini coefficient, which ranges from O for absolute equality to I for absolute inequality) tends to be stable over time within countries.[45] The study concluded that the magnitude of the poverty reduction payoff from growth depends, in part, on a country's specific circumstances and policies.

Nora Lusting and Nichols[46] revealed that the challenge of reducing poverty is indeed huge. But with out better understanding of what it takes to fight poverty and given the World's brighter economic prospects, rapid progress is feasible as long as the political will and a true spirit of partnership among governments, civil society and the private sector exist.

Jha[47] examined the empirical relationship between inequality, poverty and economic growth in India using data on consumption from the 13th to the 53rd Rounds of the National Sample Survey. The study found that a sharp rise in rural and, particularly, urban inequality and only a marginal decline in povery have characterised the post reform period. The rise in inequality is explained in terms of an increase in the relative share of output going to capital as compared to labour, a drop in the rate of labour absorption and the rapid growth of the service sector. The rise in inequality has diminished the poverty-reducing effects of higher growth. The reforms have also been characterised by widening regional inequality. This is especially true in cases of rural poverty and, to a lesser extent, also in urban poverty.

A study of Saxena[48] found that despite the good performance on the growth front, progress is reducing poverty in the 1990's has left much to be desired. Concerted policy action is needed to lift the 350 million poor, increasingly, concentrated in the poorer states, out of poverty. This requires not so much additional resources which would only result in further leakage and swelling of the already bloated bureaucracy—as better policies and sound delivery mechanisms. The focus needs to shift from maximizing of development outcomes and effectiveness of public service delivery.

A holistic approach have adopted in which the rural development programmes, the implementing agencies and attitude of the beneficiaries, all are taken together. The soundness of these three factors, should be carefully examined and oriented together to meet formidable challenges to rural development. Political withdraw from rural life and creation of a harmonious and self- sustaining rural economy personnel who should emerge from the villagers themselves.[49]

Surayan Narayana[50] analysed that there is a consensus that poverty in India has declined since the mid 1970s. This study contests this view by examining the suitability of the database and its implications for the observed trends in poverty estimates in the context of structural changes in the rural economy. It concluded that the statical estimates do not show a real reduction in poverty, but only a reduction in over estimation of poverty for the initial years followed by its underestimation for the later years.

Raghbendra Jha[51] examines the empirical relationship between economic irregularity poverty and economic growth in the Indian states, using NSS data on consumption for the 13th to the 53rd rounds. Computation of the Gini coefficient, real mean consumption and Head Count Ratio for rural and urban sectors and average for the major Indian states. The rank coefficient with across states does not usually show any tendency to fall over time. What is particularly worrisome is that the co-efficient of variation of the rural Head Count Ratio seems to be rising over time indicating greater dispersion in rural poverty across states.

Nilakantha Rath[52] analysed the poverty in rural India, the method of its measurement and its dimensions during the last three decades. He discussed the objection raised to the calorie based measurement of the poverty line. He critically examined the methods of measurement subsequently followed, over space and time. This study briefly examines the causes of the rising incidence of poverty and the policy measures to reduce it.

Environmental Degradation and Poverty

Ganesh Kumar[53] views that approximately 850 million people or one sixth of the World's population lives in the semi-arid regions of these countries. The semi-arid tropics (SAT) countries are amongst the most poor and underdeveloped countries in the world. Most people in these countries live in rural for their livelihood. The physical environment of the SAT is characterised by hot and dry climate for a good part of the year, with uncertain and limit rainfall occurring in a few months. The soil and climatic conditions in the SAT imposes a severe biophysical constraint on agriculture which manifests as a scarcity of two critical inputs for agriculture viz. erable land and water. Few crops viz, coarse cereals, pulses, oilseeds and cotton are naturally situated for cultivation in the SAT. These include changes in the cropping pattern in favour of commercial crop at the expense of coarse cereals, environmental degradation, changes in the economic policy environment in these countries.

Guruprasad Rao and Nanda Kumar[54] reported that 532 acres of agricultural land was contaminated by tannery effluent from 45 tanneries of Ranipet, North Arcot district of Tamil Nadu. About10,000 acres of agricultural land was seriously affected by tanneries of North Arcot district and 30,000 acres of land was moderately affected in Variyambadi, Ambutoor, Vellore, Dindigual, Ranipel, Vishram and Timur Township areas. The cultivable land in North Arcot district was declined from 68,000 hectares to 22,000 hectares due to tanneries.

Seth[55] revealed that watershed management has to become a people's movement, technologies would have to be simple, low cost and should be based on vegetation measures, which are self-regenerative. Claims are being made that watershed management would ensure supply of water to every field, remove hunger and poverty from poor areas, provide green cover over denuded areas, bring in more rains and improve environment. Watershed management is also described as a programme that holds the key to solve problems of employment economy, ecology, export and equity.

Rajeswaran[56] evaluated the impact of DPAP in Kamarajar district and inferred that the soil and moisture conservation scheme implemented under DPAP in dry lands helped the farmers to bring more area under crops and resulting in increased income and labour use pattern.

A study of Jean Dreze[57] found that the poorer sections of the farming community benefit very little, if at all from price support measures, consider for instance small farmers of Orissa. These farmers typically sell little grain, if any, on the market, instead they tend to combine subsistence farming with labour migration and other income earning activities that allow them to buy non-food commodities. Hence, higher food prices do not help them. What would help them is on improvement in productivity, based for instance on technological innovation and crop diversification.

Swaminathan[58] study focused that the agricultural progress will determine India's economic and political future. We can shape this future in a desirable direction through synergy among technology, public policy and farmer's co-operative action. If such synergy can be achieved, India can become the far most among the nations of the world in "farm power". If our agricultural progress is halted or revised through appropriate or adequate public policies and research priorities, social disintegration will be the result. The prosperity of the virtual world and the misery of the real world can not co-exist for long.

Rammandhar Reddy[59] suggested that the solution to the problems of Indian agriculture lies less in giving it a greater export orientation and more in increasing crop productivity (through better agricultural, research, restoring agricultural extension services and raising public investment), improving economic management and last but not least, restructuring the social relations in much of rural India. Global markets are inherently volatile and do not pass easily with the livelihood character of Indian agriculture and the domestic food security concerns. Turning Indian agriculture outwards is likely to create new and more problems rather than solve the existing ones.

Diversification becomes necessary for developing countries since growing of basic staples such as cereals can alone support economic development, notwithstanding the need to ensure food security to the people. In essence, diversification to commercial crops commodities becomes an essential strategy that can increase incomes in agriculture, minimize risks due to crop failure and above all earn foreign exchange. Valid conclusion were drawn from the data analysed regarding the change in cropping pattern and its effect on food security.[60]

Thandavakumari[61] pointed out that in the context of rural India, sustainable development aims at eradicating poverty, ensuring sustainable income along with equity, ensuring clean air, water, soil and surroundings, enabling people to enjoy material comforts with social cohesion. Integrated Rural Development based on watershed management desires great potential by the fact that it ensures the participation of the people through the stages of planning, implementation, monitoring and evaluation. The watershed committee has undertaken the initiative many new activities like planting trees in common lands, maintenance of the structures, (check dams, gully plugs etc.) maintenance of hand pumps. Understanding the benefits and needs for continuing these facilities, the committee has been working in a full-fledged manner. This indicates that the committee is fully empowered to follow further development activities in a sustainable and self-reliant manner.

Jagannath Pati[62] made a study on women, environment and sustainable rural development. The study revealed that in rural areas the depletion of natural resources by environmental degradation has a significant effect on the daily life of a woman and the well-being of her family. As more people are competing for dimishing resources, women find that in search of water, fuel wood and other forest products for their basic needs. This extra distance not only adds to their physical burden, but also means that there is less time for them to look after the family and for the preparation of food. Environmental degradation also denies other basic needs of women. Plants that provide framework and thatching material become more difficult to find as the processes of deforestation and desertification.

Prasad Rao[63] made a study on agricultural growth and poverty alleviation in Andhra Pradesh. This study brings—

out land-saving technological changes associated with irrigation getting equal importance to rural population growth in accounting for the rural poverty. High rate of agricultural production in the rural areas has been associated with low irrigation, low level of agricultural income, low wage rate and high incidence of rural poverty and not so much with high population growth or greater increase in number of growing population. Technological change in irrigation and crop production was the most important positive factor in protecting the increase in the net sown areas, by contributing to the reduction in rural poverty through the rise in agricultural incomes and wages. Rural poverty results in the availability of cheap labour as means for satisfying the rising demand for irrigation.

Erik[64] viewed that the desertification produces poverty. The declining productivity of dry—zone crop lands and range lands has its most severe impacts on scores of millions of the world's most wretchedly poor especially the villagers of semiarid Africa and South Asia. Depending quite directly on the soil and forests about them, these people see their prospects for a better life dry up along with the natural resource base.

The natural resources of the land and their environment and consumption patterns are often held responsible for ever increasing material comforts of the economically effluents which leads to severe stress on the environment while the consumption patterns of the poor are unsupportable in terms of land used and causes degradation by the poor in their slight for survival. But the rich with no such compulsion have reply to control their consumption patterns if the global environment is to be preserved. It is extremely necessary to focus attention on the development that is human centred and supports the growth of the goods and services needed for improving the welfare of mankind.[65]

Oberai *et al.*[66] emphasises in particular the function of migration in the transformation of rural and urban economies and the effects of migration on production, agriculture productivity, technological change, population growth structure and level of employment and unemployment and income distribution between the rural and urban areas. The study also includes an analysis of migrants perceptions, exceptions and experiences as characteristics of non-migrants, potential migrants and return migrants within this framework.

A study of Swarn Lata Arya[67] revealed that agriculture, animal husbandry, forestry and horticultural components of the project proved to be economically justifiable. The study also revealed the generation of employment opportunities to the extent of 70,606 man-days for casual and 2,08,606 man-days for regular labour over a period of 24 years which will be further helpful in checking the outflow of migration from the rural to the urban areas in search of livelihood. Finally, the land use pattern revealed a decline in the area of under wastelands and an increase in the area under irrigated agriculture, forestry and horticulture

Vinden Vincent[68] concluded that many hill irrigation programmes have helped the poor. There are many poor and under privileged people interested in or involved with irrigation in the hills and muntains. Naturally, it would be said if irrigation is seen as too costly or unpredictable as an area of assistance in hills. The real challenge is to find the administrative arrangements to provide assistance wanted in mountain locations as also the appropriate technologies.

Guy Pfeffermann[69] found that a strong relationship exists between the quality of the business environment and long-term national economic performance including the pace of poverty reduction. Enforcement of the rule of law in particular, the extent to which government enforce contracts between private parties is crucial to long-term development and as already noted, affects the poor as well as effluent members of society. The property rights(especially those of the poor) is highly correlated with long term economic and social progress. The efficiency of government in delivering services is also associated with economic progress.

Paul Cashin, *et al.*[70] concluded that the cross country studies appear unlikely to yield much more useful information about the effects of micro economic policies on poverty unless the dynamic effects of these policies are appropriately considered. Greater pay-offs are likely to be obtained by conducting studies based on regional or national survey data for periods encompassing clearly identifiable macroeconomic shocks. However, the number of developing counties for which reliable surveys are currently available, is relatively limited. Data collection efforts are undertaken to remedy this deficiency and it may greatly contribute to our knowledge about the links between macro economic policies and poverty reduction.

The study of Madusudhan Ghosh[71] estimated the relationship between rural poverty and the specific factors. The study also suggested that the incidence of rural poverty can be reduced significantly by increasing productive employment in the rural areas and by maintaining the real wage rate of a reasonable level. It's incidence can also be reduced by increasing the average size of the marginal and small operational holdings through land reforms. Alternatively, this can be achieved by increasing their land productivity by providing agricultural inputs including credits at subsidised rates.

Prakash Mehta *et al.*[72] made a study on poverty and farm size in India. The study considered only crop income and have not included income from animal husbandry, off farm employment, orchards etc. to arrive at the correct income level which is relevant for determining the population living below poverty line. The study discussed capital formation on selected farms in Kongra district of the state, the aspect which has not been remotely related to this study.

Thamas Palakudy *et al.*[73] pointed out that the agricultural policy should address itself not only to issues of growth in production, but also of distribution of what is produced. It should not be confined to the well being of just a few sections of the rural society, but the welfare of the entire community. This study seeks to betterment of the deprived section of society and the promise its recommendations hold for the rural poor.

The past studies reviewed in this chapter pave the way for undertaking the present study in backward region of Tamil Nadu.

PROFILE OF THE STUDY AREA

This section explains a brief of the study area, namely Virudhunagar, Tuticorin and Tirunelveli Districts. The profile includes location, administrative set up, area, population, literacy, labour force, agriculture, industry and other infrastructure facilities. The profile of the sample block and selected village panchayats in each district is also presented in this section. The study area is exhibited in Table 1.1.

Table 1.1: Study Area in Tamil Nadu

District	*Sample Block*	*Selected Village Panchayat*
Virudhunagar	Aruppukottai	Kovilangulam
Tirunelvei	Tenkasi	Veerakeralam Pudhur
Tuticorin	Srivaikundam	Srivalkundam

Source: Computed from primary data.

Virudhunagar District

Virudhunagar district was formed suitably named after the freedom fighter and Bharatha Ratna, Thiru. K. Kamaraj formerly the Chief Minister of Tamil Nadu. The Kamarajar district started functioning since 15th March, 1985. The headquarter of the district is Virudhunagar. Recently, it has renamed as "Virudhunagar District".

Location

Virudhunagar district is situated in the southern part of Tamil Nadu. It is surrounded by Madurai district on the north, Sivagangai district and Ramanathapuram district on the north east, Tirunelveli district and Tuticorin district on the south and the Western Ghats on the West.

Agriculture and Irrigation

The economy of the district is predominantly agriculture.

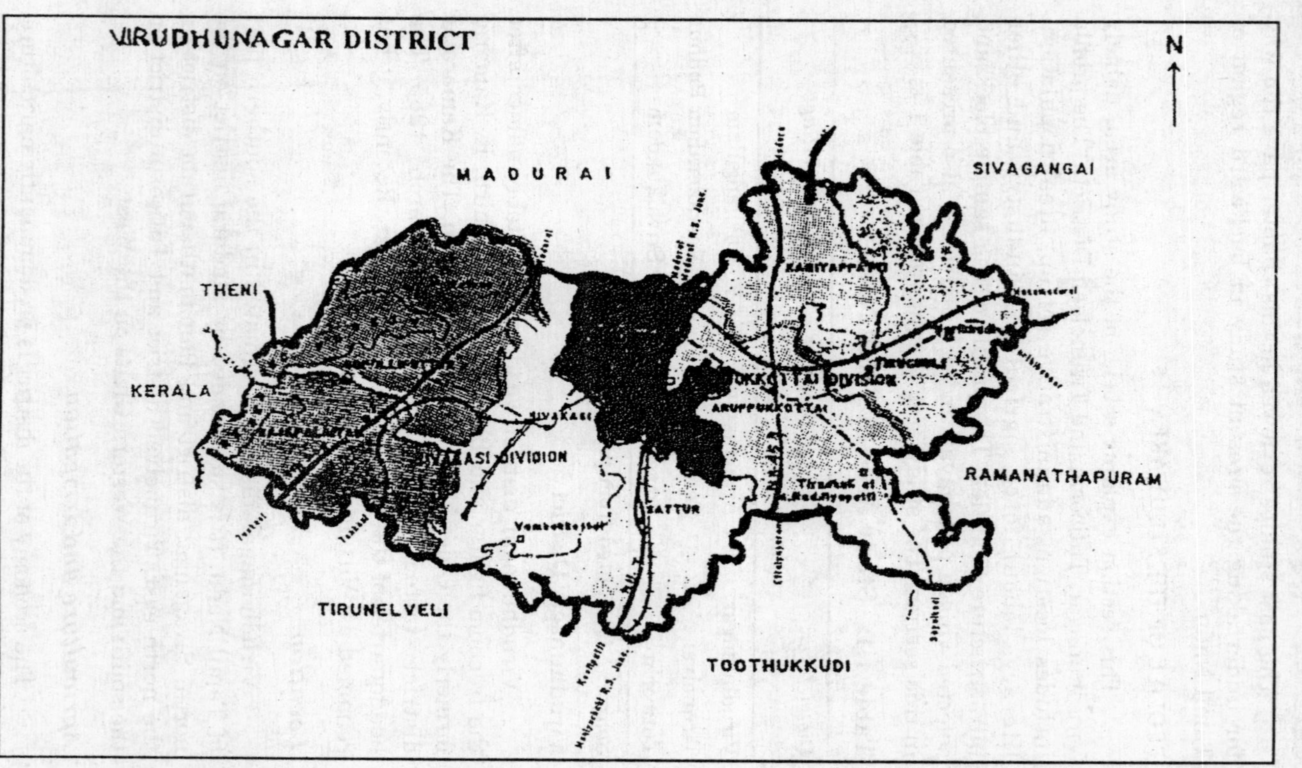
VIRUDHUNAGAR DISTRICT
N
MADURAI
SIVAGANGAI
THENI
KERALA
RAMANATHAPURAM
TIRUNELVELI
TOOTHUKKUDI
SIVAKASI
SIVAKASI DIVISION
SATTUR
KARIYAPPATTI
TIRUCHULI
ARUPPUKKOTTAI DIVISION
ARUPPUKKOTTAI

The 67.1 per cent of the total population of the district is dependent on agricultural occupation. A half of the geographical areas of the district is utilised for cultivation and net area sown is 120810 hectares. The gross area is 219352 hectares.

Soil

The soil type of the district is black soil. The run off in these soils may vary from 20 per cent to 50 per cent depending upon the rainfall. The north east monsoon period from October to December is the main rainy season. The district gets the average annual rainfall about 817 m.m.

Administrative Set up

For administrative convenience, the district has been divided into two Revenue Division such as Aruppukottai and Sivakasi. Sivakasi covers Srivilliputhur, Rajapalayam, Watrap, Sallur, Sivakasi and Vembakottai Blocks. Aruppukottai division covers Virudhunagar, Aruppukottai, Kariapatti, Tiruchily and Narikudi Blocks. The district has 11 blocks, namely, Rajapalayam Aruppukottai, Srivilliputhur, Sivakasi, Sattur, Virudhunagar, Tiruchuli, Watrap, Vembakottai, Kariapatti and Narikudi. Among all the blocks, Virudhunagar is a leading block as it is in the capital of Virudhunagar district. There are 6 Municiplalities, 10 Town Panchayats, 464 Village Panchayats and 614 Revenue Villages in the district. The district comprises six taluks, namely, Srivilliputhur,. Rajapalayam, Sivakasi, Sattur, Virudhunagar, and Aruppukottai.

Area and Population

The district covers an area of 4288 square kilometers or 1655.6 square miles. According to 2001 census the population of the district is 15,65,037. Of this total population 7,84,912 (50.12 per cent) are male and 7,80,125 (49.88 per cent) are female. The population of Scheduled Castes and Scheduled Tribes consists of 2,91,879 persons, accordingly 18.65 per cent of total tribal population. The density of population of the district is 365 persons per kilometer.

Occupational Distribution

The total labour force in the district is 7,75,821 persons which is 47.28 per cent of the total population. Of the total labour force, 36.86 per cent are cultivators, 22.25 per cent are agricultural labourers and 8.03 per cent are engaged in livestock, forestry, fishing and allied agricultural activities. Thus, 66.6 per cent of workers are engaged in agricultural sector. The remaining 33.4 per cent are engagea in cottage household industries, trade and commerce and other activities.

Industries

The importance of industrial development of Virudhunagar district has to be viewed against the background of the twin characteristics of the area:

(i) It is dry district with a low annual rainfall, with not fertile soil for agricultural purposes and no perennerial river water potential.

(ii) The population of the district have a low standard. They are living and living by very hard work, often migrating to more prosperous neighboring district, quite often to far away places as well.

There are 49 large -scale industries, 438 small scale industries, 287 tiny sector sheds in Virudhunagar district. The large scale industries are textile mills, cement, paper, printing and electrical industries. A large number of small scale industrial units are engaged in the production of safety matches which accounts for one third at all the India output. Other important lines of activity of the small scale industries in the district are labels for fireworks, printing inks, tin containers, playing cards, black insulation tapes, spring washers, domestic utensils, furniture, soap, fountain pens and nibs, etc.

Transports

The district has well developed a net work of roads, rail links connecting all the important centers within the district as well as various commercial centers of neighbouring districts. The district is connecting by one National Highway (NH7) with outlaying areas. The existing total length of metallic roads is 425.6 kilometres. The non-metallic road is 643.7 kilometer and the kutcha road is 393.7 kilometer. The 56.8 per cent of the villages in the district are accessible by pucca roads.

Infrastructure

All the villages in the district can not claim to have drinking water facilities. Power supply and educational facilities are available in 98.3 per cent and 88.2 per cent of the villages respectively. Marketing, medical, post and telegraph facilities are available only in 3.3 per cent, 19.5 per cent and 34.9 per cent of the villages respectively.

Literacy

Virudhunagar District has a low per cent of literacy compared with other districts of Tamil Nadu state, 54.19 per cent of literacy is heartening. The literate population of the district is 8.48,217 persons. There are 1030 elementary schools, 168 higher elementary schools, 133 higher secondary schools, 11 Arts Colleges, 12 Polytechnics and 2 Industrial Training Institutes, 2 Engineering College and 145 Adult Education Centres in the district.[74]

Aruppukottai Block

Aruppukottai block is located in the South-eastern region of the Virudhunagar district. It is bounded on the west by Virudhunagar block, on the north by Kariapatti block, on the east by the Trichuly block and on the south by Tuticorin district. The block has an area about 326.39 square kilometers.

The total population of the block is 1,62,572 persons. Cent per cent of the population of this block is rural in character. The Scheduled Castes and Scheduled Tribe as cover 11.7 per cent of the total population. The density of the population of the block is 317 persons per square kilometers.

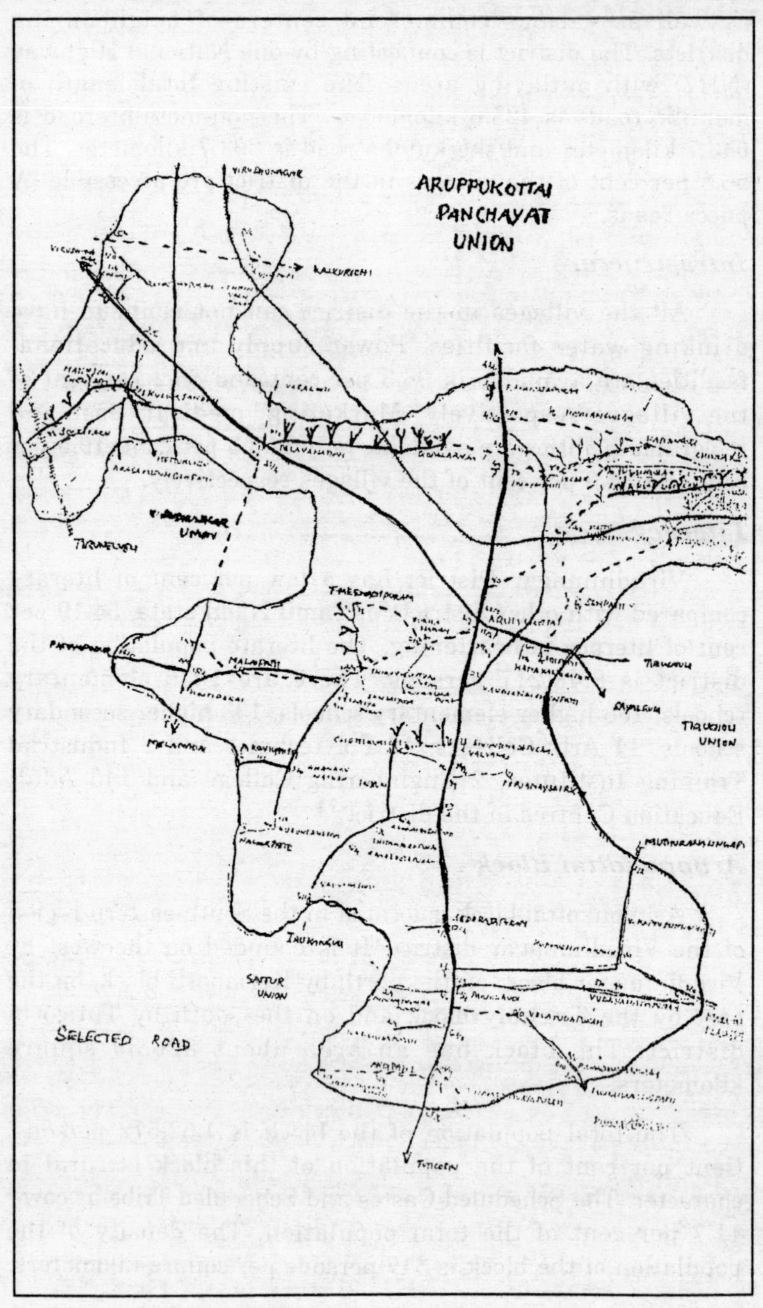
ARUPPUKOTTAI
PANCHAYAT
UNION
KALKURICHI
SATTUR
UNION
SELECTED ROAD

There is one town panchayat, 41 revenue villages and 74 inhabited villages in the Aruppukottai block. The total labour force in the block constitute 46.16 per cent of the total population. Of the total workers, 19.19 per cent are cultivators, 42.24 per cent are agricultural labourers, 16.10 per cent are engaged in livestock, forestry, fishing and allied agricultural activities. Thus, 77.53 per cent of workers are engaged in agricultural sector. The remaining 22.47 per cent of workers are engaged in cottage household industries, trade and commerce and other activities such as mining, quarrying construction, transport, storage and communication etc.

Aruppukottai educational division includes Trichuly, Aruppukottai and Sattur taluks. There are 435 primary schools, 61 middle schools, 21 high schools in the Aruppukottai division, 98 primary and middle schools are functioning in the Aruppukottai block.

All the villages in the block are electrified. The block has 25 kilometers of metallic road, 11 kilometers of non-metallic road and 26 kilometers of Kutcha road. The total length of the railway tracks in the block is 16 kilometers,. There are 15 post offices covering 74 villages and 11 telegraph offices covering 32 villages in the block.

The net cultivated area is 26,546 hectares which is 81.3 per cent of the total area of the block. There is no area under forests and 20.3 per cent of the total area are not available for cultivation. The uncultivated area and current fallow lands constitute 2.3 per cent and 7.7 per cent of the total area respectively.

The net area irrigated in the block is 2,723 hectares which is 10.25 per cent of irrigated area to net area sown. Of the net area, 1132 hectares are irrigated with wells, 117 hecatres with canals and 1474 hectares with other sources of irrigation.

The gross cropped area in the block is 27,639 hectares and 1093 hectares are under double/multiple cropped area. The food crops like paddy, millet, ragi etc. are cultivated in 27.5 per cent of the gross cropped area. The area under

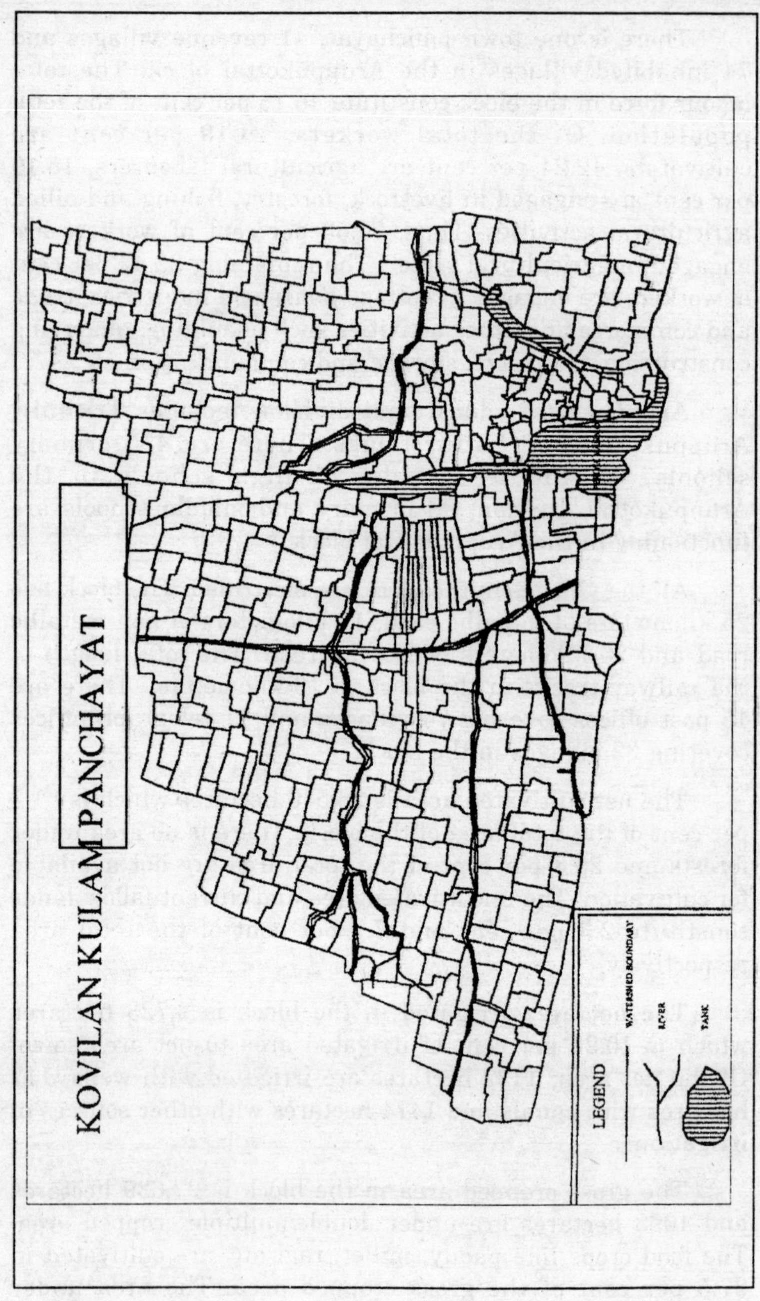
KOVILAN KULAM PANCHAYAT
LEGEND
WATERSHED BOUNDARY
RIVER
TANK

commercial crops like groundnut, sugarcane, cotton, chillies, etc., are cultivated in 57.58 per cent and other crops are cultivated in 14.9 per cent of the area in the block.

The Aruppukottai block covered 32 village panchayat, namely Amanakkunatham, T. Meenakchipuram, Thiruviruthalpuram, Vellaiyapuram, Kurundahmadam, Vadhuvarpatti, Pokampatti, Gopalapuram, Kovilangulam, Ramanujapuram, Kattangudi, Sempatti, Puliyooran, Kanjanaichenpatti, Athipatti, Sukkilenatham, Chettikurichi, Periyanayagipuram, Chidamparapuram, Chettipatti, Sethurajapuram, Pandalgudi, Velayuthapuram, Koppuchittampatti, Thummakundu, Palevanatham, Periyavallikulam, Soolakarai and Kullorsandai.[75]

Kovilangulam Village Panchayat

Kovilangulam village panchayat is located in Northern part of Aruppukottai Block. The village covers of 1173.14 hectare of area. A half of the geographical area of the village panchayat is utilised for cultivation. Irrigated area is 1069.46 hectare and waste land is 86.38 hectare. The cultivable land is 683.41 hectare. The population of the block is 2700. Of this total population, 1300 are male and 1400 female. The economy of the district is mainly agriculture (75 per cent), industry work (20 per cent) and other (5 per cent).

The main crop cultivated in this village, panchayat is cholam, cotton, etc. The remaining crops are paddy, cumbu, pulses, etc. The soil type of the village panchayat is Red Soil. The livestock are also available in (buffalo, cow and cattles) in Kovilangulam village panchayat.[76]

Tirunelveli District

Location

Tirunelveli district is located in the south eastern part of Tamil Nadu. But for Kannyakumari district, this is the southern most district and is bounded by Virudhunagar district in the north, Tutocorin district on the cast, Gulf of Mannar and Kannyakumari district on the South and Western Ghats and Kannyakumari district on the West. It

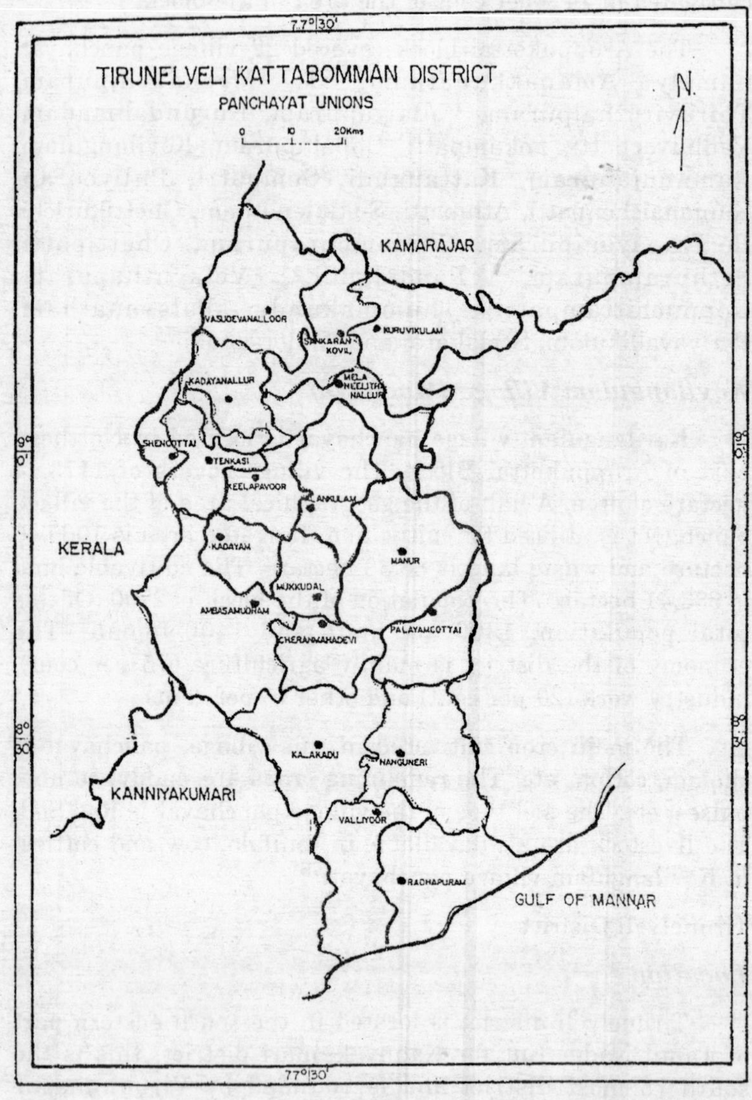
77° 30'
TIRUNELVELI KATTABOMMAN DISTRICT
PANCHAYAT UNIONS
0 10 20Kms
N.
KAMARAJAR
VASUDEVANALLOOR
KURUVIKULAM
SANKARAN KOVIL
MELA NEELITHA NALLUR
KADAYANALLUR
9° 0'
SHENCOTTAI
TENKASI
KEELAPAVOOR
ANKULAM
KERALA
KADAYAM
MANUR
MUKKUDAL
AMBASAMUDRAM
PALAYAMCOTTAI
CHERANMAHADEVI
8° 30'
KALAKADU
NANGUNERI
KANNIYAKUMARI
VALLIYOOR
RADHAPURAM
GULF OF MANNAR
77° 30'

lies between 8.05' and 9.30' of the northern latitude and 77 05' and 78 25' of the eastern longitude.

Administrative set up

The district extends over an area of 6,42,728 hectares accounting for 4.95 per cent of the total area of Tamil Nadu. The district comprises of seven taluks, namely, Radhapuram, Nanguneri, Ambasamudhram, Shenkottai, Tenkasi, Palayamkottai and Tirunelveli Taluks. The Tirunelveli district comprises of 3 revenue divisions and 19 Panchayats, namely, Palayamkottai, Melaneelithanallur, Kurvikullam, Sankaram Koil, Vasudevannallur, Kadayanalur, Tenkasi, Senkottai, Alangulam, Cheranmadevi, Manur, Kalakkadu, Nanguneri, Valliyoor and Radhapuram. There are 5 Municipalities namely, Palayamkottai, Melapalayam,Kadaiyanallur, Puliyankudi and Tenkasi.

Population

According to the census of 2001, the total population of the Tirunelveli district is 24,93,189. The density of population per squares killometre is 366. The population in the rural area is 17,02,468 (68.28 per cent) and that of the urban area is 7,90,721 (31.72 per cent). The population consists of 12,24,319 male (49.11 per cent) and 12,68,870 female (50.89 per cent). The total number of Scheduled Caste in the district is 4,47,654 (17.96 percent) and scheduled tribes is 8792 (0.35 per cent). Of this scheduled tribes, 9.77 per cent (877) are living in the hill forest areas and they are called as "Kanikaran" and "Paliyans".

The vital rates are as follows. Birth rate:21, Death rate: 81. Infant mortality rate: 59.0 and Meternal Mortality rate: 21.The age at marriage is 25.7 for male and 20.0 for female. The average age of acceptors are 31.8 for Vasectomy (Spouse), 28.1 for tubectomy nad 25.9 for I.V.D.

Occupation

Of the total workers, nearly, 25 per cent (2.51 lakhs) are cultivators while 29 per cent are engaged as agricultural labourers. Thus, 54 per cent of workers are engaged in agricultural sector. The remaining 46 per cent are engaged in non-agricultural activities.

Agriculture

The district has more than one third (38.5 per cent) of its total geographical area under cultivation. Of the net area sown, 18.9 per cent of the area is cultivated more than once. The important food crops grown in the district are paddy, maize, ragi, millet and black gram. The commercial crops like cotton, chillies, groundnut and coconut are also grown. Paddy is the main crop covering 1,56,463 hectares accounting for 30 per cent of the gross cropped areas of 5,24,311 hectares.

Of the total area irrigated, (1,74,534 hectares/40 per cent of the net areas sown) wells cover 67,664 hectares, tanks feed 84,124 hectares. Cannels irrigate 21,953 hectares and the remaining 793 hectares are under other sources of irrigation.

Climate and Rainfall

The district's climate may be said to be equable. The maximum temperature is rarely above 108 F and the minimum seldom below 80F. The most drying period in the district is the months of April and May and the lowest temperature is often recorded during January. The normal rainfall for Tirunelveli is 814.8 m.m.

Rivers and Soils

The river Tamiraparani, rises from Agasthiyar Malai in Pothigai hills in the Western Ghats passes through Ambasamudram, Tirunelveli, Srivaikundam and Thirunchedur taluks and enters between Tuticorin and Thiruchendur. The best irrigated lands in the district lie on either side of this river. The rest of lands are dry and undulating. Major types of soil found in the district are black loom, black sandy loom, red loom, and red sandy loom. The district is endowed with good deposits of limestone, graphits, granite stone, garnets and, gypsum and salt bitten.

Forest

The height of the Western Ghats in the Tirunelveli district, ranges from 3000 to 5000 feet situated the western boundary. Well clothed with forest containing magnificent and valuable trees between elevations of 1500 to 3000 feet, it shoots upto 6000 feet in certain places.

Industries

Industrially, the district is fairly developed. There is a concentration of industries in Tirunelveli taluk. The District Industries Centre was established in Tirunelveli on 1.7.78 to provide service and facilities to small industries, tiny industries, cottage and village industries.

Of the 24 large scale units, 15 are textile mills, the rest manufacture cement, steel drums, papers and pulp and chemicals. There are 2,386 small scalè industrial units with an estimated annual production of Rs. 7.25 crores and total employment of 30,600 persons.

Transport and Communication

The district has a good network of road connecting important towns and villages. It served a network of rail link of 312 kms in length. The Broad-guage railway opened in 1990 connects Tiurnelveli with the neigbbouring Kannyakumari and Trivandrum districts. This should bring the greater economic development to the district. The communication facilities are also adequate in the district. There are 944 post office, 242 telegraph offices and 4,112 telephone connections.[77]

Tenkasi Block

Tenkasi Block is located in the western area of the Tirunelveli district. Shenkottai block form western boundry of this block, Kadayanallur block is in the north and Ambasamudram block is the southern boundary of this block. Kilapavoor block is the eastern boundary of the block.

There are 14 village panchayats, namely, Aryapandi, Karukkupilaivalasai, Kasimayanpuram, Kuthukalvalasai, Mathalamparai, Pattakurichi, Periyapillaivalasai, Piranoor, Pattapattur, Chillasaipunavoo, Sumaithethapuram, Thempothai, Thiruchitarampalam and Vallam in Tenkasi Block. There are 5 Town panchayats, namely, Ilanji,

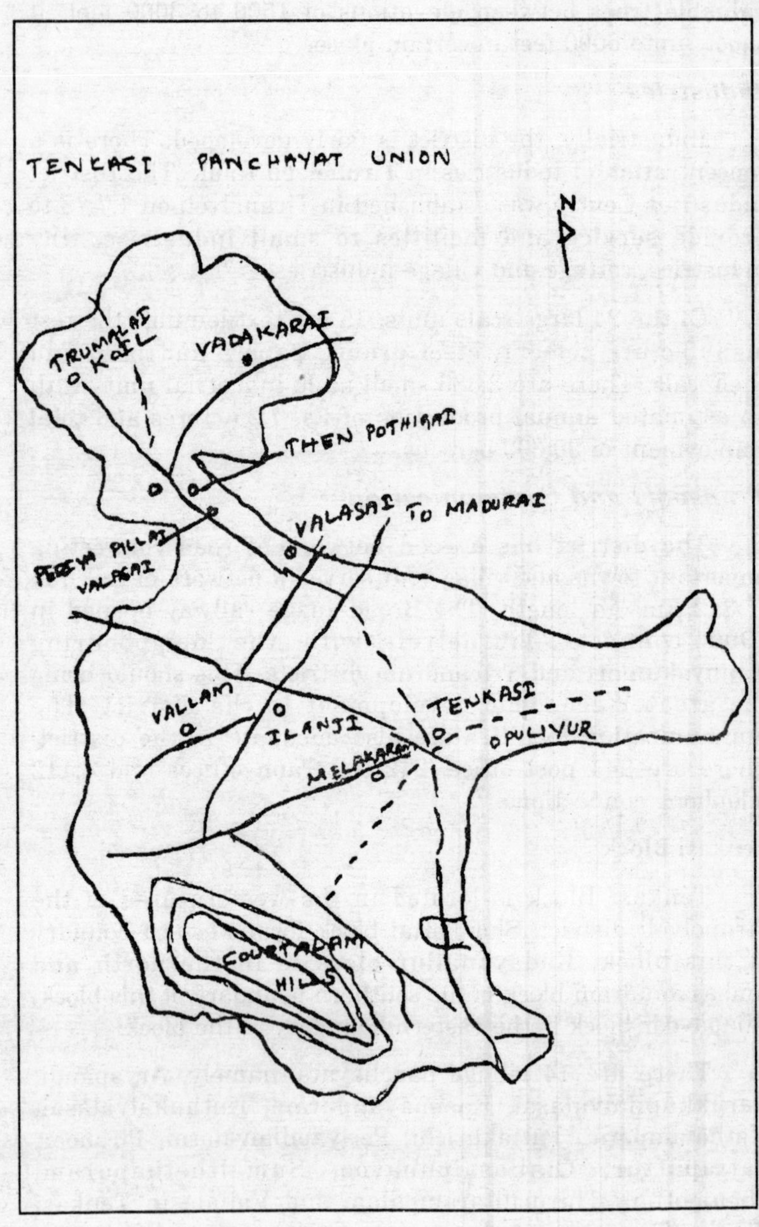
TENKASI PANCHAYAT UNION
N
TRUMALAI KOIL
VADAKARAI
THEN POTHIRAI
VALASAI
TO MADURAI
PERIYA PILLAI VALASAI
VALLAM
ILANJI
TENKASI
PULIYUR
MELAKARAM
COURTALAM HILLS

Melagaram, Panpoli, Sundarapandiyapuram and Vadakarai. The Tenkasi block comprises of 24 Revenue villages.

The total population of this block is 78,665. Of this total population, 24,372 (30.98 per cent) persons are living in urban area and the remaining 54,293 (69.02 per cent) persons are living in rural area in this block. The total population comprises 39,111 male and 39,554 female and it accounts for 49.72 per cent and 50.28 per cent respectively. The Scheduled Caste and Tribe forms 18,364 which is 23.34 per cent of the total population of the block.

Of the total working force (30,427), cultivators form 25.8 per cent, i.e., 7850 persons, 9161 agricultural workers form 30.11 per cent of the total workers. The remaining work force engaged in breeding, forestry, fishing, cottage and household industries, trade and commerce.

The infrastructure development is in a better condition at Tenkasi block. Electricity power supply available for the block as a whole. The length of the metallic road is 954 kms and the non-metallic road is 41.4 kms. The number of villages connected by kutcha road is 10 number. Almost all the villages are given the facilities of post and telegraph.

In Tenkasi block, paddy and chillies are cultivated during the period of April to August. Pulses and groundnut are cropped during the period from September to December in dry lands. During June and July, Ragi are cultivated in the block. The river, namely, Chittar which is used as irrigation and drinking water sources in this block.

There are 4 important cooperative production societies in the block.They are: Cane and Bamboo Society, Visvanathapuram, Glazzad Rottery Cooperative Society, Thanpathani, Carpentry and Block Smithy unit, Tenkasi and Brick cooperative Industries Society, Panpuzhi.

There are 17 commercial bank in the Tenkasi block and it covers 13 State Bank of India, 2 Regional Rural Banks and 1 District Central Cooperative Bank, 16 Primary Agricultural Credit Societies.[78]

Veerakeralam Pudur Village Panchayat

Verakeralam Pudur village is located in eastern part of Tenkasi Block. The village covers an area of 605.23 acre and the cultivated land of 601.44 acre. Of this total land, 474.44 acres are wet land and 127.77 acres are dry land. The population of the village is 4499.Of this population, 2231 are male and 2268 are female. The main crop production of this village panchayat is Paddy, Chillies, Onions, Cotton,etc.

The total labour of the village is 3363 persons. Of this total, 2879 are agricultural labourers and 484 persons are other workers. A3/4 of the geographical area of the village panchayat are utilised for cultivation. The type of soil found in the village panchayat are black sandy loom. The percentage of literacy is 54. The source of irrigation is tank and canals. The village panchayat covered the village of Thayarthoppu, Rajapandi, Surandai, etc.[79]

Tuticorin District

Location

Tuticorin district carried out of the eastwhile Tirunelveli district in 1986 has certain rare features. The mixed landscape of the sea and the 'their' (waste) lands has imbibed some special traints in the character of sons of the soil. Valor land devotion with burying patriotism are the watch words of the people here. The story of our country freedom struggle can be completed without mentioning the supreme sacrifices of the illustrations of the district like V.O.C. Pillai who brought the first Swadeshi ship 'Galia' to the Tuticorin port and Veerapandi Kattabomman who waged a war against the British. The peoples poet Subramania Bharathi and the revolutionary Vanchinathan were also the proud sons of the soils.

Administrative Setup

The area of the district is 4621 square kilometers. The district has three revenue divisions, eight Taluks, 12 Blocks, 2 Municipalities, 20 Town Panchayats, 468 Revenue village and 7 Constituents. The 12 Blocks are: Thoothukudi,

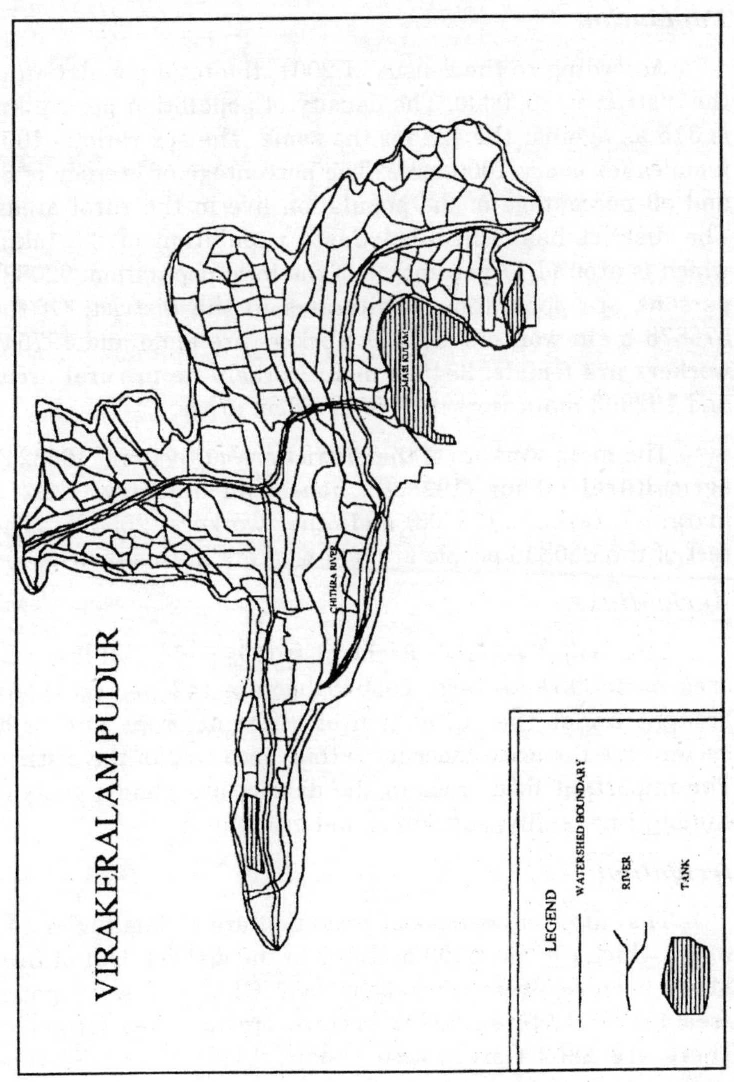
VIRAKERALAM PUDUR
CHITHRA RIVER
MASI KULAM
LEGEND
WATERSHED BOUNDARY
RIVER
TANK

Srivaikundam, Karunkulam, Tirunchendur, Uthangudi, Alwarthirunagari, Sattankulam, Ottapidaram, Kovilapatti, Kayattar, Vilathikulam, Pudar.

Population

According to the census of 2001, the total population of the district is 1500000. The density of population per sq. km is 315 as against the 428 for the same. The sex ratio is 1051 females for every 1000 male. The percentage of literacy is 63 and 59 percentage of the population live in the rural areas. The district has Scheduled Caste population of 2.5 lakhs which is around 17 percentage of the total population. 920887 persons are population as literates in the district. Of the 576878 main workers, 379331 workers are male and 197547 workers are female. 384525 main workers lie in rural areas and 192353 main workers live in urban areas.

The main workers of the district are cultivators (108824), agricultural labour (192836), household industry (21321), marginal workers, (28706) and other workers (253897). The rest of the 850336 people are non-workers in this district.

Agriculture

The main food crops in the district is paddy. Of the total area of 450954 hectare, 185048 hectare (42 per cent) are brought under the cultivation of different crops and 5190 hectare are the area under more than once crop of the district. The important food crops in the district are paddy, cholam, cumbu, ragi, chilly, sugarcane and groundnut.

Irrigation

The different sources of irrigation are canals tanks and wells, which covers 45199 hectares in the district. Out of this, 21941 hectares were covered by well. Of the gross irrigated area(45199 Hectare), 39492 hectare are net area irrigated. There are 2852 Government canals, 1420 tanks, 473 tube wells and 21947 other wells in the district. The river Tamirabarani comes from the Western Ghats passes through this district.

Industry

In this district, 982 factories are working factories. There are 238 trade unions, 1051 small scale industries. The main industries are SPIC, TAC, STERLITE, HWP, DCW, etc. Large number of small scale industries are producing chemical items for various uses. The district has covered by the sea shore and salt also produced in most of the area of the district.

Cooperation

The district has 3 Primary Land Development Banks, 1 District Cooperative Bank, 8 Urban Banks, 157 Primary Agriculture Credit Societies, 32 Workers Cooperative Societies, 59 Employees Cooperative Societies and 27 Primary Cooperative stores.

Transport

Tuticorin district is having National Highway of 112.4 kilometres, State Highway of 64.498 kilometers and Corporation and Municipality road of 191.725 kilometers. One seasport and one Airport are also important Transport for the development of the district. Three railway connection are available from Tuticorin to the Northern State.[80]

Srivaikundam Block

The type of soil found in the block are sandy soil lands (7900 hectare), clay (39795 hectare), Alkaline (1300 hectare). The block is covered with yield land by the watershelter.

The town panchayat of the Srivaikundam includes Srivaikundam, Sayer puram, Earal and Perunkulam blocks. The Srivaikundam blocks covers by 31 village panchayas namely Agaram, Aniyepasenallur, Arumugamangalam, Idayarkadu, K. Appankoil, K.Kashpa, Varadarajapuram, Korkeai, Kottarakurichi, Kovangadu, Managalakurichi, Manjal Neerkayal, Maramanagalam, Mukkani, Nattahi, Bathmanapamanagalam, Palaygalal, Parakkiramapandi, Perur, Sirunthonda Nallur, Sivakalai, Soolaivaikkal, Srimoolakkasai, Sripasangusanallur, Thiruppanisettikulam, Thiruppuliyenkudi, Tholappannai, Umarikaadu, Valavallan, Vellore and V.Athichanallur.

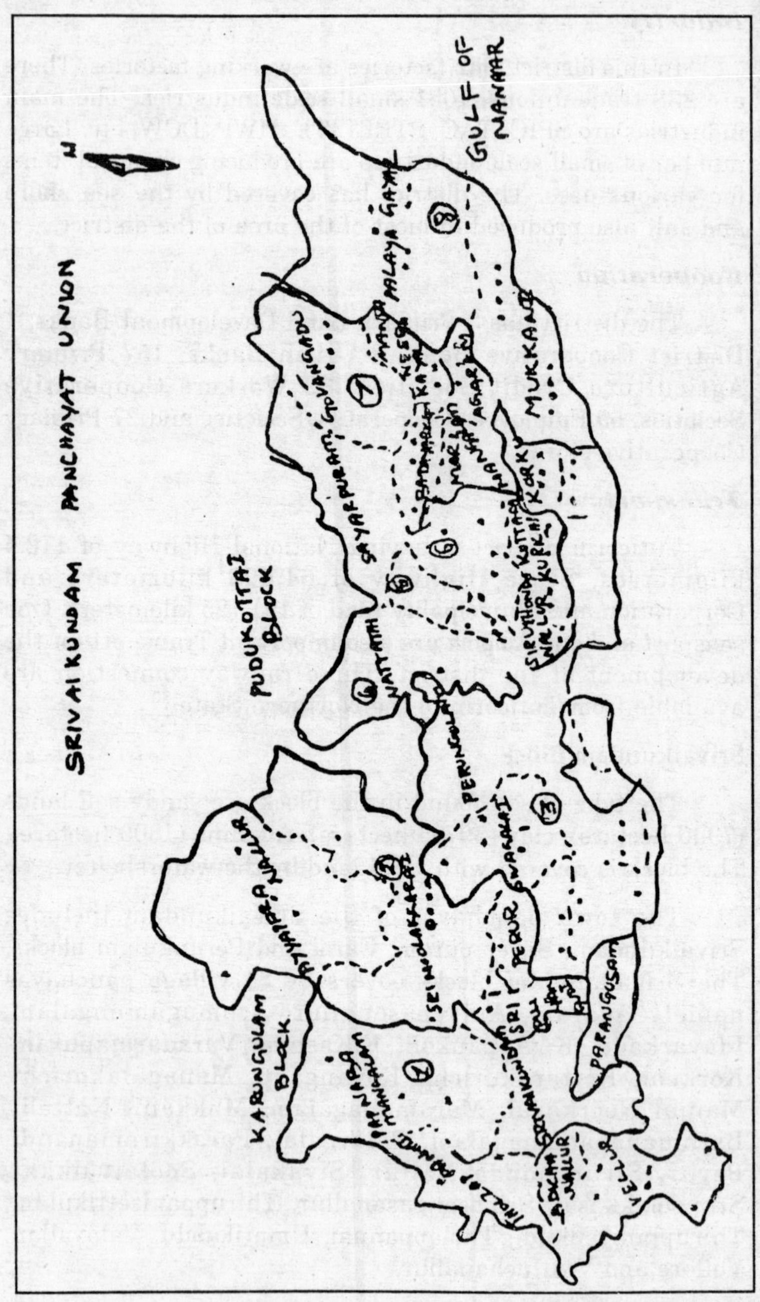
SRIVAIKUNDAM PANCHAYAT UNION
PUDUKOTTAI BLOCK
KARUNGULAM BLOCK
GULF OF MANNAR
N

The total area irrigated is 14,228,55 acre. The food crops like, paddy, plantain and pulses are cultivated in this block. The total population of the Srivaikundam block is 71723 persons. The population consists of 34763 male and 36960 female. The total number of Scheduled Caste in the block is 19590 persons and Schdeuled Tribe is 178 persons.[81]

Srivaikudam Village Panchayat

The total area of land of Srivaikudam village panchayt is 693.70 hectare. There are 13 villages in the panchayat namely, i.e. Indira Nagar, Nagan Colony, Muthalesswaren Colony, Munner Colony, Kadaniyan Colony, Pettuthraisamy puram, Kalangudi, Lakshmi Puram, Srivaikundam, Pitchivathoppu, Kaniyon kalany, Parunanithi Nagar, Kosalram Nagar.

Srivaikundam is one of the rural areas of Thoothukudi district. It is land where Tamaraparani/Porunai river flows gracefully. It is the only river with its beginning and ending within the boundaries of Tamil Nadu. The river starts from Pothigai hills and ends it in Bengal sea.

Srivaikundam is also famous due to the birth place of Arulmigu Kumara Guruparar who was born in the early period of 17th century and is worshipped as the poetic religions and philosophical saint. His contributions to Tamil literature as well as Saivam are of great value. Thoottukudi Sarvodaya Sangam has seven branches. Among the seven branches, one branch is located in Srivaikudam.

The section presented the brief profile of Virudhunagar District, Aruppukottai block, Kovilangulam Village panchayat, Tirunelveli District, Tenkasi block, Veerakeralam Pudur Villager Panchayat, Tuticorin District, Srivaikundam block, Srivaikundam Village Panchayat, are guiding to analyse the Environmental Degradation and Poverty in South Tamil Nadu.[82]

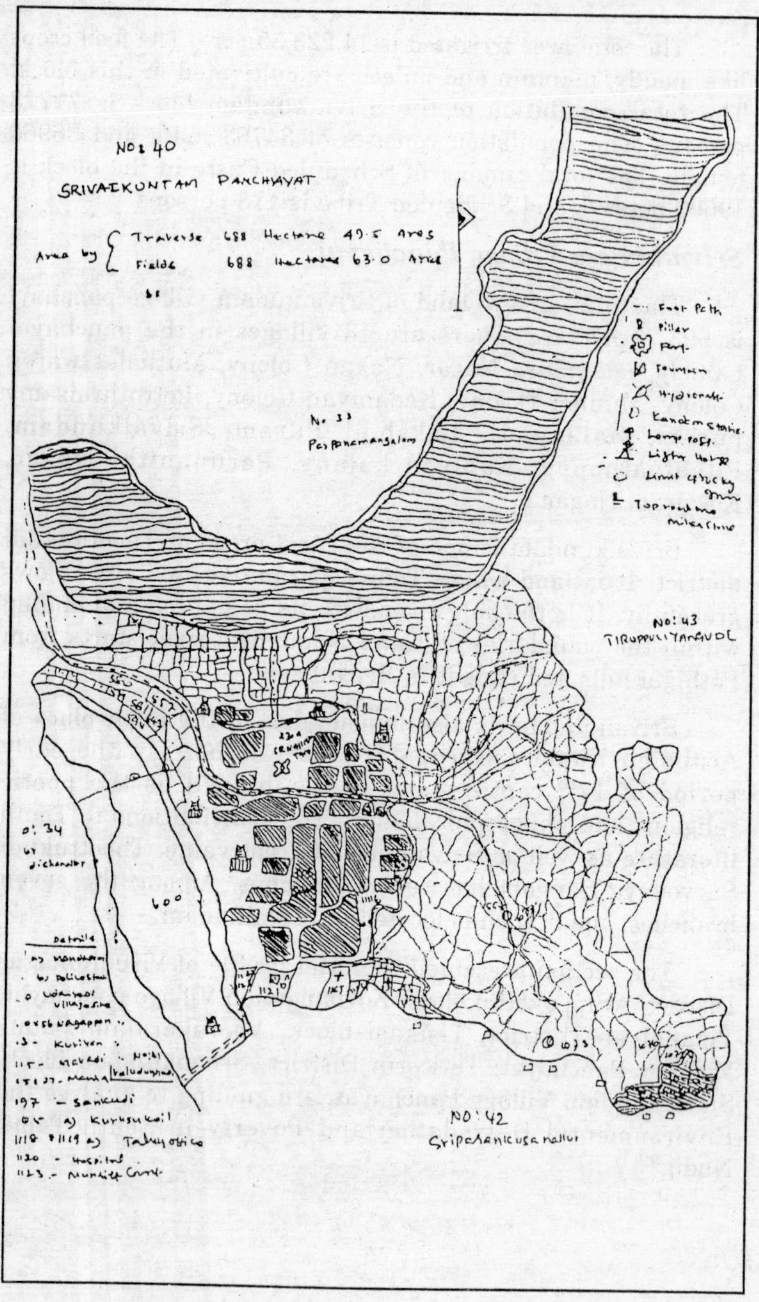
NO: 40
SRIVAIKUNTAM PANCHAYAT
Area by Traverse 688 Hectare 49.5 Ares
Fields 688 Hectares 63.0 Ares
Foot Path
Pillar
Fountain
Lamp Post.
Light House
No. 33
No: 43
TIRUPPULIYANGUDI
0: 34
600
Details
NAGAPPAN
Kuriyan
Valudugham
197 – Sankudi
Kurusukoil
1118 & 1119 Taluq office
1120 – Hospital
1123 – Munsiff Court
NO: 42

REFERENCES

1. Jose Jacob, "Effectiveness of Irrigation Projects in Kerala, *Yojana*, Vol. 37, No. 5, March-31, 1993, pp. 8-10.

2. Attar Singh, *"Environmental Degradation in Food Prone Areas"*, Pointer Publisher, Jaipur, 1991.

3. C. Rammanohar Reddy, "Watershed Development: Economic Power", *The Hindu Survey of Environment,* 1997, pp. 209-213.

4. Sankaram Ayala, "Eco-Technology Focus for Sustainability in Farming", *The Hindu,* Dec. 7, 2000.

5. S.V. Murugan and *et al.,* "Sustainable Agriculture Importance in the Context of Environmental Degradation and Population Explosion", *Peninsular Economist,* Vol. XI, No. 1, 1998-99, p. 181.

6. S. Ganesamoorthy, "Sustainable Development and Environment Role in Land use", *Peninsular Economist,* Vol. XI, No. 1, 1998-99, pp. 77-98.

7. KasthuriBhai Dhanasekaran, "Agricultural Technology and Sustainable Development", *Peninsular Economist,* Vol. XI, No. 1, 1998-99, pp. 89.

8. P.K. Muthukumar and Rajendran, "Voluntary Organization and Sustainable Development of Water Resources", *Peninsular Economist,* Vol. XI, No. 1, 1998-99 pp. 181-82.

9. M.S. Rajeev, and *et al.,* "Crop sequences with Patton Rice: A Way for Sustainable Agriculture in Flood Prone Areas", *Peninsular Economics,* Vol. XI, No. 1, 1998-99, pp. 114-115.

10. R. Chinniah *et al.,* Groundwater Management Problems, *Peninsular Economist,* Vol. XI, No. 1, 1998-99.

11. C. Karthikeyan *et al.,* "Economic Utilization and Conservation of Rural Environment Resources", *Peninsular Economist,* Vol. XI, No. 1, 1999-93.

12. Jitendra Kumar Sinha, "Drought: Causes and Remedies", *Kurukshetra,* Vol. 48, No. 12, September, 2000, pp. 30-34.

13. Navin Chandra Joshi, "Land Reforms through Wasteland Development", *Kurukshetra,* Vol. 48, No. 12, September, 2000, pp. 17-20.

14. Dhulasi Brirundha, *"Environmental Degradation and Management Strategies in India",* Paper Presented in UGC

Seminar on Issues in Environmental Management and Planning at Sri G.V.G. Visalakshi College for Women, Udurnalpet, Jan. 25, 2001.

15. K.S. Gopalakrishnan, P. Sakthivel and R. Sunilkumar, Geomophometric Study of the Kodayar Rivers Basin in Western Ghat Regions of Kanyakumary District Tamil Nadu," *National Geographical Journal of India,* Vol. 43(4), Dec. 1997, pp. 295-306.

16. Noor Mohammad, Agricultural Development and Environmental Degradation in Sonipat District, Haryana. *National Geographical Journal of India,* Sept. 1997, pp. 198-208.

17. Nigar Ajyam. Environmental Degradation of Abdullahpur: Meerut District. *National Geographical Journal of India,* Vol. 43, June-1997, pp. 163-166.

18. R. Pramanik, K. Sarkar and V.C. Joy, "Role of Destrivoir Soil Arthropods in Nutrient Release as Affected by Pesticide Contamination," *Pollution Researchmuch,* Vol. 19, No. 1, 2000.

19. T.S. Chouhen, *"Global Status of Land Degradation and Desertification: A Study of Causative Natural and Anthropogenic Factors"* Vol. II Printweel Publishers Distributors, Jaipur, 1998.

20. G. Emtiazi, "Dolorisation and Biodegradation of dyes by Asper Gillus Terrenes Grown in Wheat Straw with in Peroxides Activity", *Environ Media,* Vol. 19(1): 2000. pp. 31-35.

21. R.G. Desai, *"Agricultural Economy"* Himalaya Publishing House: Mumbai 1998. pp. 85-90.

22. R.K. Sivanappan, "Land and Water use for the Future", Kisan World, Vol. 20, No. 11, 1993. p. 45.

23. Isaac Arnon, *"Modernization of Agriculture in Developing Countries"* John Wiley and Sons Ltd. New York, 1987, p. 40.

24. Ashok K. Mitra, *Planning and Management of Surface Irrigation in Drought—Prone Areas",* Gokulae Institute of Politics and Economics, Pune, 1987, p. 147.

25. Yu Xiaogang, "Conflict in Resource Management for Ecosystem Services", Water in Lashi Watershed, Lijiang, *Economic and Political Weekly,* Vol. XXXVI, No 30, July 28, August 3, 2001, pp. 2851-58.

26. Wang Qinghna, "Forest Management and Terraced Agriculture: Case Study of Hani of Aibo Mountains, Yunnan" *Economic and Political Weekly*, Vol. XXXVI, No. 30, July 28, August 3, 2001.

27. A.R. Padoshri, "Land Resource Management; A Case Study of Goa, Oxford & IBH Publishing Co. Pvt. Ltd., New Delhi, 1992.

28. Kanachana Chopra, "The Management of Degraded Land: Issues and Analysis of Technological and Institutional Solutions:", *Indian Journal Agricultural Economics,* Vol. 51, No. 1 to 2, Jan-June 1996, pp. 238-247.

29. A. Vaidyanathan, "Depletion of Groundwater Some Issues", *Indian Journal of Agricultural Economics*, Vol. 51, No. 1 and 2, Jan.-June 1996, pp. 184-192.

30. Chandrama Goswami, "Land use and Environment: A Study". *Southern Economist,* Vol. 40, No. 1, May, 1, 2001, pp. 25-26.

31. B.P. Singh, "The Eastern Himalaya: Net Lands Forests and Beliefs", *Economic and Political Weekly,* Vol. XXXVI, No. 31, August 10, 2001, pp. 2968-75.

32. Normen Uphoffeno, *et al., "Managing Irrigation, Analysing and Improving Performance of Bureaucracies"*, Sage Publication India Pvt. Ltd., New Delhi, 1996.

33. S.L. Dhyani *et al.*, "Economic Analysis of Watershed Management Programme in Outer Himalaya: A Case Study of Operational Research Project", *Indian Journal of Agricultural Economics,* Vol. XVIII, April-June 1993, pp. 237-95.

34. N. Nagaraj, M.G. Chandrakanth *et al.,* "Borewell Failure in Drought-prone Areas of Southern Indian: A Case Study", *Indian Journal of Agricultural Economics,* Vol. VIIX, No. 1, Jan-March 1994. pp. 101-106.

35. A.P. Srinivasamoorthy, *"Irrigation Planning in India",* Himalaya Publishing House, Bombay, 1990.

36. B.D. Dhawan, *"Studies in Minor Irrigation with Special Reference to Ground Water"*, Commonwealth Publishers, New Delhi, 1990.

37. A.K. RajulaDevi, "Food Poverty and Consumption among Landless Labour Households", *Economic and Political Weekly,* Vol. XXXVI, NO. 28, July 15, 2001, pp. 2656-64.

38. A. Vadyanathan, "Poverty and Development Policy" *Economic and Political Weekly,* Vol. XXXVI, No. 21, May.26-June 1, 2001, pp. 18047-22.

39. Danny M. Leipziger, "The Unfinished Poverty Agenda why Latin America and the Caribbean Lag Behind", *Finance and Development,* Vol. 38, No. 1, March 2001, pp. 38-41.

40. R.K. Ghosh, " NGO Intervention in Poverty Alleviation: Scope and Reality", *Kurukshetra,* Vol. 49, March, 2001, pp. 2-9.

41. World Development Report 2000/2001, *"Attacking Poverty: Overview",* World Bank, Washington, D.C. 2001.

42. Vankatesh, "Experiments with Poverty in Andhra Pradesh and Rajasthan". The Hindu, December 12, 2000.

43. Deepa Narayan, "Poverty is Powerlessness and Voicelessness" *Finance and Development,* Vol. 37, No. 4, December, 2000, pp. 18-21.

44. Masood Ahmed and Hugh Bredenkamp, "Supporting Poverty Reduction in Low-Income Developing Countries: The International Community's Response", *Finance and Development,* Vol. 37, No. 4, December 2000, pp. 10-13.

45. Dani Rodrik, "Growth Versus Poverty Reduction: A Hallow Debate", *Finance and Development,* Vol. 37, No. 4, December 2000, pp. 8-9.

46. Nora Lusting and Nicholas Stern, "Broadening the Agenda for Poverty Reduction: Opportunity, Empowerment, Security", *Finance and Development,* Vol. 37, No. 4, December 2000, pp. 3-7.

47. R. Jha, "Reducign Poverty and Inequality in India; Has Liberalization Helped?" *Economic and Political Weekly,* Vol. 35, No. 11, March 200.

48. N.C. Saxena, "How have the Poor? Mid Term Review of Ninth Plan," *Economic and Political Weekly,* Vol. XXXV, No. 41 October 7, 2000, pp. 3627-30.

49. Bepin Behari, "Adopt Holistic Approach to Fight Poverty, *Kurukshetra,* Vol. 39, October 1991.

50. M.H. Suryanarayana, Hou Real is the Secular Decline in Rural Poverty, *Economic and Political Weekly,* Vol. 35, No. 24, June 17, 2000.

51. Raghbendra Jha, "Growth, Inequality and Poverty in India, Statical and Temporal Characteristic" *Economic and Political Weekly,* Vol. 35, No. 12 March 11, 2000.

52. Nilakantha Rath, "Poverty in India Revisted, *"Indian Journal of Agricultural Economics"* Vol. 51, Nos. 1 and 2, Jan.-June, 1996, pp. 76-107.

53. A. Ganesh Kumar, *"Future of Agriculture in the Semi-Arid Tropics",* Project Sponsored by the International Crop Research Institute for the Semi-Arid Tropics (ICRISAT) Patanchu, Hyderabad, 2000.

54. Guruprasad Rao and Nanda Kumar, "Impact of Tannery Effluents on Seed Germinability and Chlorophyll Content in Sizer Arientium" *Population Research 2;* 1983-89.

55. S.L. Seth, "Watershed Management in India", *Kurukshetra,* Vol. 48, No. 9, June 2000, pp. 2-7.

56. R. Rajeswaran, *"Critical Analysis of the Functioning of Drought Prone Area Programme",* Unpublished M.Sc. (Agri) Project, 1984. Tamil Nadu Agricultural University, Coimbatore.

57. Jean Dreze, "Storving the Poor-I," *The Hindu,* February 26, 2001, p. 12.

58. S. Swaminathan, "Shaping our Agriculture Future", *The Hindu*, January 11, 2001, p. 12.

59. C. Rammandhar Reddy, "Agriculture Plight", *The Hindu*, December 23, 2000, p. 12.

60. N. Jeganathan, "Diversifying Cropping Pattern and Food Security in Tamil Nadu", *Peninsular Economist,* Vol. XI, No. 1, 1998-99.

61. K. Thandavakumari, "Sustainable Development and Environment Management through Integrated Watershed Programme", *Peninsular Economist*, Vol. XI, No. 1, 1998-99, pp. 62-69.

62. Jagannath Pati, "Women, Environment and Sustainable Rural Development", *Kurukshetra*, Vol. 5. No. 5, October 2000, pp. 22-27.

63. Prasad Rao, "Agricultural Growth and Poverty Alleviation: A Study in Andhra Pradesh" *Indian Economic Panorama,* Vol. 10, No. 2, October, 2000, pp. 53-60.

64. Erık, "Poverty, Population Growth and Desertification", T.S. Chouhan (Ed.), Global Status of Land Degradation and Desertification, Printweel Publishers and Distributors, Jaipur, 1998, pp. 472-78.

65. Pradeep Chaturdevi, "World Renewable Energy Network. Sustainable Development the only Route of Prosperity to poor", *Environment of People,* Vol. 7, October, 2000.

66. A.S. Oberai and A.K. Manmohan Singh, *"Causes and Cousequences of International Migration",* Oxford University Press, Bombay, 1983.

67. Swarn Lata Arya et al., "Economic Viability of Watershed Management Project Selected to Rehabilitate Degraded Aravali Footkills of Zharyana", *Indian Journal of Agricultural Economics,* Vol. 49, No. 4, Oct-Dec, 1994, pp. 591-600.

68. Vinden Vincent *"Hill Irrigation, Water and Development in Mountain Agriculture: Inter Mediate Technology"* Overseas Development Institute London, U.K. 1995.

69. Guy Pfeffermann, "Poverty Reduction in Developing Countries: The Creole of Private Enterprise". *Finance and Development,* Vol. 38, No. 2, June 2001, pp. 42-45.

70. Paul Cashin, et al., "Macro Economic Policies and Poverty Reduction", *Finance and Development,* Vol. 38, No. 2, June 2001, pp. 46-48.

71. Madusudhan Ghosh, "Agricultural Development and Rural Poverty in India", *Indian Journal of Agricultural Economics,* Vol. 51, No. 3, July-Sept. 1996, pp. 374-78.

72. Prakash Mehta and Anjala Kumari, *"Poverty and Farm Size in India",* Mittal Publications, New Delhi, 1990.

73. Tharmas Palakudy and Sukhpal Singh, "The New Agricultural Policy and the Rural Poor", Social Action, Vol. 43, No. 3, July-September, 1993, pp. 328-223.

74. Office Records, District Collectorate, Virudhunagar, 2002.

75. Office Records, Panchayat Union, Aruppukottai, 2002.

76. Office Records, Village Panchayat Kovilankulam, 2002.

77. Office Records, District Collectorate, Tirunelveli, 2002.

78. Office Records, Panchayat Union, Tenkasi, 2002.

79. Office Records, Village Panchayat, Veerakeralam Pudur, 2002.

80. Office Records, District Collectorate, Tuticorin, 2002.

81. Office Records, Panchayat Union, Srivaikundam, 2002.

82. Office Records, Village Panchayat, Srivaikundam, 2002.

2

Environmental Degradation and Rural Poverty

The root cause of environmental degradation in India can be attributed to rapid growth of population in India. It has approximately 18 per cent of World population but only 2 per cent of the geographical area. The application of medical knowledge and social care has lowered the death rate while the birth rate remains fairly constant. Dandekar has analysed the pattern of decline in the death rate and birth rate for the period 1972-78 and 1979-90 and observed that the death rate was declined greater during the second sub period (1979-90) than in the first sub-period (1972-78). However, in contrast to the decline in the death rate, the decline in the birth rate during the second sub-period was much smaller than in the first sub period.

Due to this, poverty could not be eradicated in spite of the fact that poverty alleviation is on the national agenda for more than fifty years. In 1972 in the Stockholm Conference on Environment, then Prime Minister of India Smt. Indira Gandhi has said that poverty is a great pollutant. Twenty years later in 1992 World Bank stated that "Poor are the agents and victims of environmental degradation". The poor become agents of environmental degradation when they are victims of it.

Poverty may be considered as the most profound social trap. Social traps area situations in which the short term, local optimizing of individuals goes a foul. In this sense, they indicate imperfection in the unregulated free market approach to resource allocation, which relies on short term, local optimising of individuals. Social traps abound in environmental issues because of the absence of well defined property rights and the pervasiveness of environment externalities. Social traps are analogous to what has become known as the "tragedy of the common" in which there is breakdown or absence of institutional mechanisms for co-operation and the resolution conflicts between individual and community interests in the management of Common Property Resources.

The debt crisis has been a factor influencing many of the environmental problems experienced by developing countries today. The crisis has its origin in the events of 1970's. During this period many developing countries attempted to narrow the gap between themselves and the industrialised countries. To finance the imports of machinery and technology the developing countries often borrowed money from the Banks and Governments in the industrial countries.

Many developing countries have turned to their debts and have chopped down forests, embarked on large scale open cast mining or accepted toxic waste in an attempt to obtain these additional resources to meet debt repayments. The poverty that national debt creates in these countries can not be calculated. Nor can it be separated from any initiatives to improve the environment. The poor in urban and rural areas who are deprived of access to adequate housing water and sewage facilities are caught in a vicious circle of poverty and environmental deterioration.

Probably no other group is more affected by environmental destruction than poor village women. Every dawn brings with it a long march in search of fuel, fodder and water. It does not matter if the women is old, young or pregnant: Crucial household needs have to be met day after day. As ecological conditions worsen, the long march becomes ever longer and more tiresome. Caught between poverty and environmental destruction, poor rural women in India could well be reaching the limits of physical endurance.

The specific difficulties that women face-their extraordinary work burden or lack of access to health care, for instance—do not arise out of ecological deterioration per se. They are pocketed in the sexual division of labour, marked by a double work burden (at home and outside) and by the specific nature of the task they do, and in the unequal distribution of resources like food within the household, which stems from women's inferior status in the household and from a lack of control over cash and productive resources like land. But given this situation, environmental destruction further increases women's already acute problems in a way very different from those of men. It is worth mentioning, that they have lessee access and less control over resources surrounding them. The World Women, whose way of life is intrinsically linked with the environment bear the burnt of the environment's destruction and, for reasons beyond their control, poor women frequently become the agents of their own resource depletion as they struggle to ensure the survival of their families.

The present chapter is divided into two parts. The first part analyses the poverty in India and in Tamil Nadu. The second part analyses of environmental situation, monsoons and causes of environmental degradation at central and state level especially in Tamil Nadu. The analysis deals with degraded land, irrigation land, cropping pattern and intensity, cultivable land, uncultivable land, net area sown, agriculture yield/ production, utilisation of fertilisers and pesticides, etc.

POVERTY

Poverty has persisted, despite all our rhetoric, even after 50 years of effort in tackling poverty, more than 200 million remain poor by any measure, reforms required the dismantling of a policy regime often justified in the mane of the poor it also involves significant changes in relative prices of various goods and relative profitability of different sectors. This was bound to have an impact on poverty. The poverty line was defined at 1960-61 prices to be Rs. 20 per person per month for urban areas and Rs. 15 for total areas, enough to provide 2250 calories in urban and 2400 calories in rural area per day.

Conceptually, "Poverty is a result of low levels of assets, coupled with low returns on the assets. Almost by definition, the poor have very few assets to draw on beyond their own labour. In addition to being deprived of critical material assets of land, they also lack education, skills and health in addition to such public assets such as community infrastructure, basic services and government programmes. In this sense they suffer from poverty of access to public goods and service".

Poverty Line

The simplest measure of poverty is the Head Count Ratio' (HCR) which represents the percentage of the population that earns/spends below a certain level of income (expenditure). This level is identified as the poverty line. HCR is estimated on the basis of household expenditures collected by the NSSO through nationally representative sample surveys. Direct income has been used to compute HCR primarily because of the dearth of data on a regular basis. NCAER has for the first time in India collected direct income data from nationally representative sample surveys. In the recent past NCAER has collected different income data through the Rural Economic Demographic Survey of 1980-81, Market Information Survey of Households beginning 1985-86 on an annual basis, now through its first Human Development Indicator Survey, 1994.

The poverty line for rural India as a whole is Rs. 2,444 per capita per year. The percentage of the population below the poverty line is estimated as 39 in 1994. Poverty is highest in Orissa (55 per cent), West Bengal (51 per cent) and Himachal Pradesh (45 per cent). The incidence of poverty is low in Andhra Pradesh, Haryana, Punjab, and Kerala.

The mean household income of the poor has worked out be Rs. 1,591 per annum. The Head Count Ratio among the annual income of less than Rs. 20,000 category is 69, and in the Rs. 20,001-40,000 category is 13 per cent. The HCR declines substantially as landholding size increases. The HCR is only 16 per cent among STs and the lowest is 27 per cent among Christians and both literate groups. The incidence of poverty is highest among both the lower and upper segment below poverty line groups.

According to the World Development Report, 1990, more than one billion people in the developing World are living in poverty. Of this, about 420 million poor are in India alone; 80 per cent of are in rural areas. According to the Human Development Report of UNDP, (1997) the 44 per cent of India's population lives in absolute poverty today. Nearly one third of the World's poor lives in India which occupies as the 47th rank in poverty among 78 countries.

The poverty line in various states of India is given in Table 2.1.

Table 2.1: Levels of Income and Poverty Line by States of India

Regions / States	*Poverty line (Rs. / Year)*
Haryana	2,818
Himachal Pradesh	2,818
Punjab	2,818
Bihar	2,535
Uttar Pradesh	2,557
Madhya Pradesh	2,324
Orissa	2,330
Rajasthan	2,623
North-eastern Region	2,775
West Bengal	2,642
Gujarat	2,418
Maharashtra	2,338
Andhra Pradesh	1,654
Karnataka	2,241
Kerala	2,922
Tamil Nadu	2,370
All India	2,444

Source: Economic Survey, 2002.

Poverty Level in India

The percentage of population below the specified poverty line is a measure of the incidence of poverty, that is, how many are poor. Sen's measures are not adaptively decomposable overpopulation subgroups. A measure advanced by Foster, Greer, and Thorbecke (FGT) in 1984 in adaptively decomposable apart from satisfying the desirable properties suggested by Sen.

The mean household income of those below the poverty line is Rs. 1,591 per annum which is only 33 per cent of the overall per capita income of Rs. 4,485 for Rural India. This income is around one quarter of the per capita incomes of Punjab, Karnataka, Maharashtra, and Gujarat, and over 40 per cent of that of Orissa, Kerala, and Madhya Pradesh. The intensity of poverty, as measured by the Sen's Index, was found to be alarmingly high in the states that registered higher incidence of HCR and Gini. The states of Haryana, Maharashtra, Andhra Pradesh, and Punjab registered a lower Sen Index than the national average. Similarly, Orissa, Uttar Pradesh, Kerala and Rajasthan have a higher Sen's Index largely due to the wider disparity of income among the poor which is a matter of concern.

Orissa and West Bengal have almost one quarter of their rural households in the lower segment below the poverty line. Andhra Pradesh has the least number of households in this category. This is a manifestation of lower levels of consumer price index reported from Andhra Pradesh. However, it is apparent that even in Haryana and Punjab over 10 per cent and 14 per cent of households, respectively, live in abject poverty. Earlier it was stated that the average household wage income (both agricultural and non-agricultural) in Haryana and Punjab is not the highest among the states mostly because of the number of person days of work at least in the case of agriculture. Thus we may assume that the landless wage earners in Haryana and Punjab are as poor as their counterparts in other states.

Table 2.2: Poverty Level for States of India

Regions / States	*Poverty*	*Indices*
	Sen	*FGT*
Haryana	0.11	0.03
Himachal Pradesh	0.23	0.09
Punjab	0.15	0.05
Bihar	0.21	0.08
Uttar Pradesh	0.22	0.09
Madhya Pradesh	0.15	0.05
Orissa	0.30	0.12
Rajasthan	0.20	0.08
North-eastern Region	0.12	0.13
West Bengal	0.24	0.09
Gujarat	0.19	0.07
Maharashtra	0.13	0.04
Andhra Pradesh	0.08	0.02
Karnataka	0.18	0.08
Kerala	0.13	0.04
Tamil Nadu	0.16	0.06
All India	0.18	0.07

Source: Economic Survey, 2002.

Both incidence and intensity of poverty are higher among STs and SCs in comparison with the national average. HCR in about 50 among STs and SCs in comparison with only 39 for rural India. The Sen's index in as high as 0.24 among STs and SCs in comparison with only 0.18 among the rural population as a whole. HCR is 43 per cent among the Muslims in comparison with only 27 among the Christians and 39 among the Hindus. The Sen's index was found to below only among the Christians.

However, the intensity of poverty is highest among the households classified as belonging to the lower segment below the poverty line with a Sen's Index of 0.63 and FGT of 0.33

the highest for any category of population group. These indices are 0.22 and 0.04 in the upper segment below the poverty line category levels of village development are related with poverty. Less developed village have higher HCR and also a higher Sen's Index.

Poverty Line in Southern States of India

The Planning Commission report, 2001 reveals the poverty in southern states of India, which is given in Table 2.3.

Table 2.3: Poverty Line by Southern States (1999-2000)

(Persons in lakhs)

States	*Rural* *No. of persons*	*Urban* *No. of persons*	*Combined* *No. of persons*
Andhra Pradesh	58.13	60.88	119.01
Karnataka	59.91	44.49	104.40
Kerala	20.97	20.07	41.04
Tamil Nadu	80.51	49.97	130.48
Percentage	(20.55)	(22.11)	(21.12)

Source: Planning Commission, 2001.

Table 2.3 shows the number of population below poverty line during the period 1999-2000. In southern states compared with other states, Tamil Nadu is the top most list in the number of population in below the poverty line i.e., 20.55 per cent of person in rural and 22.11 per cent of person in urban out of Indian population.

ENVIRONMENTAL DEGRADATION

The Environment can be defined as the physical surrounding of man of which he is a part and on which is dependent for his activities like physiological functioning, production and consumption. His physical environment stretches from air, water and land to natural resources like energy carriers, soil and plants, animals and ecosystems. For urbanised man, a large part of his environment is man made. But, even then, the artificial environments (building, roads) and implements (clothes, automobiles) are the result of an input of both labour and natural resources. Commonly the term 'Environment' is restricted to ambient environment. In that view, the indoor environment (home, work place) is regarded as isolated piece of environment to be treated on its own terms.

The indoor environment usually is under the jurisdiction of the public health authorities. Health risks are mainly linked to space heating, cooking and lighting. Low grade fuels, insufficient ventilation and low or non-existing chimneys are often the main problems. Additionally, there may be problems connected with moist, light, incidence, hazardous substances from building materials, lacquers and paints. Problems with drinking water, sewage and waste are not linked to the dwelling as such, but rather due to a lack of appropriate infrastructure. Statistics on indoor environment may be regarded as a subset of statistics on human settlements and the urban environment.

Environmental degradation is a complex problem which is being increasing, it faced with the pass safe of time. It has in fact, reaches an alarming state at the turn of this century when unsustainable agriculture development practice have been adopted across the country, of course, at a different level. Deforestation either for the sake of fuel, fodder and timber, or for expansion of agriculture land or both, heavy but unscientific doses of chemical fertilisers without understanding the actual requirement of the soil, irrigation use of irrigation water with mismanagement canals, extraction of underground water of the upper acquifer washed of from the deep lower acquifer through tube wells especially for irrigation purposes, over cultivation without proper rotation of crops and overgrasing of animals without understanding the potentially of pastures and grazing lands have resulted into severe environmental degradation specially the land degradation. We all feel and experience deterioration in environment condition but selection of meaningful precise indicators and to quantity them is a difficult tasks, if not impossible.

Development activities are measured in terms of national accounts which in turn are defined as production of goods and services during accounting period. However, certain environmental functions which are crucial for economic performance and generation of human welfare such as provision of natural resources now threaten the sustained productivity of the economy and economic production and consumption activities. These activities impair environmental quality by overloading natural links with wastes and pollutants. The private and social costs of the use of the natural resources and the degradation of the environment may be taken into account for the sustainable development in the conventional accounts.

Environmental Degradation in India

The present study has analysed the environmental degradation with the available data (1985-86 to 1994-95) on land use pattern, cropping pattern, soil degradation, irrigation, fertiliser use, pesticide etc.

Land Availability and Utilisation

On the basis of nine-fold land use classification the land use statistics are available for roughly 305 million hectares out of the total 329 million hectares of the total geographic area, which accounts for 93% of the total land. Recently the areas under non-agricultural uses has increased due to increases in development activities e.g. housing, transport system, irrigation etc. About 22 M.ha are occupied by the housing, the industry and for other non-agricultural uses, 19.5 M.ha are snowbound and remote, leaving only 264 M.ha for agriculture, forestry, pasture and other bio-mass production. Mostly through reclamation of old fallow and cultivable waste lands and diversion of groves. The data shows that land use in the country, over the last five decades, has undergone drastic change. Land under agriculture has almost doubled, forest cover has dwindled to less than half, large tracts of fertile agriculture and forest land have been diverted for urbanisation and settlements.

Table 2.4: Availability of land in India

Year	*Forest land availability per person (hectare)*	*Per capita availability of agriculture land in rural areas (hectare)*
1985-86	0.030	0.327
1986-87	0.090	0.311
1987-88	0.089	0.302
1988-89	0.084	0.305
1989-90	0.083	0.302
1990-91	0.082	0.302
1991-92	0.080	0.302
1992-93	0.078	0.303
1993-94	0.077	0.297
1994-95	0.076	0.291

Source: "Estimates in this table have been worked out on the basis of area figure of land utilisation published by the Ministry of Agriculture, 1996.

It is clear from the Table 2.4 that the per capita availability of agriculture land in rural areas had been declined from 0.327 hectare in 1985-86 to 0.291 hectare in 1994-95. The table 2.5 reveals that the waste land is due to non-forest degraded area and forest area degradation with high use of chemical application. Out of 1295.74 lakhs hectare of waste land, the non-forest degraded area (72.3 per cent) and forest degraded area (27.7%) were 936.85 lakhs hectare and 358.89 lakhs hectare of waste land respectively in India during the year 1996.

Consequently the overcultivation of land beyond the sustainable limit, unbalanced heavy doses of chemical fertilisers without knowing the actual deficient nutrient in the soil due to its non-testing, over irrigation and mismanagement of canals, over cultivation, excessive and unscientific use of insecticides and pesticides expansion of agricultural land on other indispensable uses of land such as forest land and so on, have resulted into ecological imbalances and degradation.

Table 2.5: Waste Land in India (Area in lakhs hectare)

States	*Non-Forest degraded area*	*Forest Degraded area*	*Total waste land*
Andhra Pradesh	76.82	37.34	114.16
Assam	9.35	7.95	17.30
Bihar	38.96	15.62	54.58
Gujarat	71.53	6.83	78.36
Haryana	24.04	0.74	24.78
Himachal Pradesh	14.24	5.34	19.58
Jammu & Kashmir	5.31	10.34	15.65
Karnataka	71.22	20.43	91.65
Kerala	10.53	2.26	12.79
Madhya Pradesh	129.47	71.95	201.42
Manipur	115.6	28.41	144.01
Megalaya	0.14	14.24	14.38
Nagaland	8.15	11.03	19.18
Orissa	5.08	8.78	13.86
Punjab	31.57	32.27	63.84
Rajasthan	11.51	0.79	12.30
Sikkim	180.01	19.33	199.34
Tamil Nadu	33.92	10.09	44.01
Tripura	1.08	8.65	9.73
Uttar Pradesh	66.35	14.26	80.61
West Bengal	21.77	3.59	25.36
Union Territories	8.89	27.15	36.04
Total	936.85 (72.3)	358.89 (27.7)	1295.74 (100.0)

Source: Forestry Statistics, 1996, Government of India

Note: Figures within parenthesis denotes percentages.

Environmental Degradation has started taking place and is manifested in loss of forest areas and cover loss of bio diversity, soil erosion, water logging, salinity and ability sinking of underground waterable, contamination of water and soil etc., which is causing great concern to the academicians, planners and decision makers. The cultivable waste land in India during the study period is depicted in Table 2.6.

Table 2.6: Cultivable waste land in India (in mha)

Year	*Cultivable waste land (in mha)*	*% of total area*
1985-86	16.60	5.1
1986-87	16.43	5.1
1987-88	16.28	5.0
1988-89	15.77	5.0
1989-90	15.00	5.0
1990-91	14.99	4.9
1991-92	14.57	4.9
1992-93	14.41	4.7
1993-94	14.26	4.7
1994-95	14.26	4.7

Source: Department of Agriculture and Cooperatives, Ministry of Agriculture, New Delhi. 1997.

Concentration of cultivable waste land was more than sub regional average in 10 state and was extremely high mountain areas due to the severe soil erosion and steep slopes

Table 2.7: Cultivable Land in India

Year	*Cultivable land (m.ha)*	*Year*	*Cultivable land (m. ha)*
1985-86	32.20 (9.89)	1990-91	30.22 (9.28)
1986-87	32.19 (9.88)	1991-92	30.05 (9.23)
1987-88	31.97 (9.82)	1992-93	29.47 (9.05)
1989-89	31.74 (9.75)	1993-94	29.07 (8.93)
1989-90	30.53 (9.37)	1994-95	29.07 (8.93)

Source: Department of Agriculture and Cooperatives, Ministry of Agriculture, New Delhi. 1997.

Note: Figures with in parenthesis denotes percentages.

land under non-agricultural uses includes area under settlements, water bodies, transport network, etc. About it the cultivable land was decreased from 16.60 million hectare to 14.26 million hectare in 1994-95 due to the development of Government project.

From 1985-86 to 1994-95, the cultivable land had decreased from 32.20 m.h. to 29.07 m.h. The variation in the cultivable land in various years depends upon the steps of slopes, ruggedness of terrain, soil fertility, amount of soil and wind erosion.

The area under current fallow land has decreased from 14.81 million hectare to 13.25 million hectare during period from 1985-86 to 1994-95, due to implementation of land development scheme by the Government of India. It is inferred that 0.6 percentage of current fallow land has decreased during the study period due to vagaries of monsoon which might keep their lands fallow.

Table 2.8: Current Fallow Land in India

Year	*Current fallow land (in mha)*	*% of current fallow*
1985-86	14.81	8.2
1986-87	14.12	8.7
1987-88	14.05	10.4
1988-89	13.96	8.0
1989-90	13.88	7.9
1990-91	13.70	7.7
1991-92	14.67	7.9
1992-93	14.15	7.7
1993-94	14.38	7.9
1994-95	13.25	7.6

Source: Department of Agriculture and Co-operation, Ministry of Agriculture, New Delhi 1997.

Soil Degradation

Soil is the non-renewable natural resource, which supports life on earth. About 130 million hectare of land (45%

of total geographical area) is affected by serious soil erosion through ravine and gully, shifting cultivation, cultivated wastelands, sandy areas, deserts and water logging (Government of India, 1989).

Soil erosion by rain and river that takes place in hilly areas causes land slides and floods, while cutting trees for firewood, agricultural implements and timber, grazing by a large capacity of grass lands, traditional agricultural practices, construction of roads, indiscriminate (limestone) quarrying and other activities, have all led to the opening of hill-faces to deserts, dust, storms, whirlwinds and destruction of crops, while moving sand covers the land and makes it sterile. Excessive soil erosion with consequent high rate of sedimentation in the reservoirs and decreased fertility have become serious environmental problems with disastrous economic consequences. Of the 16 rivers of World which experience service erosion and carry heavy sediment load, 3 rivers, namely Ganga, Brahmaputra and Kosy occupy the 2nd, 3rd, 12th position respectively. Deforestation contributes to loss of precious top soil which amount to about 35 per cent of the global sediment load going to oceans even though water flowing through our river is only about five per cent of the flow of rivers in the world.

Soil erosion results in huge loss of nutrients in suspension or solution, which are removed away from one place to another, thus, causing depletion or enrichment of nutrients. Besides the loss of nutrients from the topsoil, there is also degradation through the creation of gullies and ravines which makes the land unsuitable for agricultural production. Subsidence of the land in some areas and landslides in the hilly tracts are problems affecting highways, habitations and irrigation dams.

The use of pesticides above permissible limits enters the food chain, causing health hazards. A major concern particularly about chlorinated hydrocarbons like DDT is their persistence in soil. Among fertilizers the conversion of fertilizer—N is gaseous forms—ammonia (NH3) and various oxides of Nitrogen leads to atmospheric pollution. Escape of

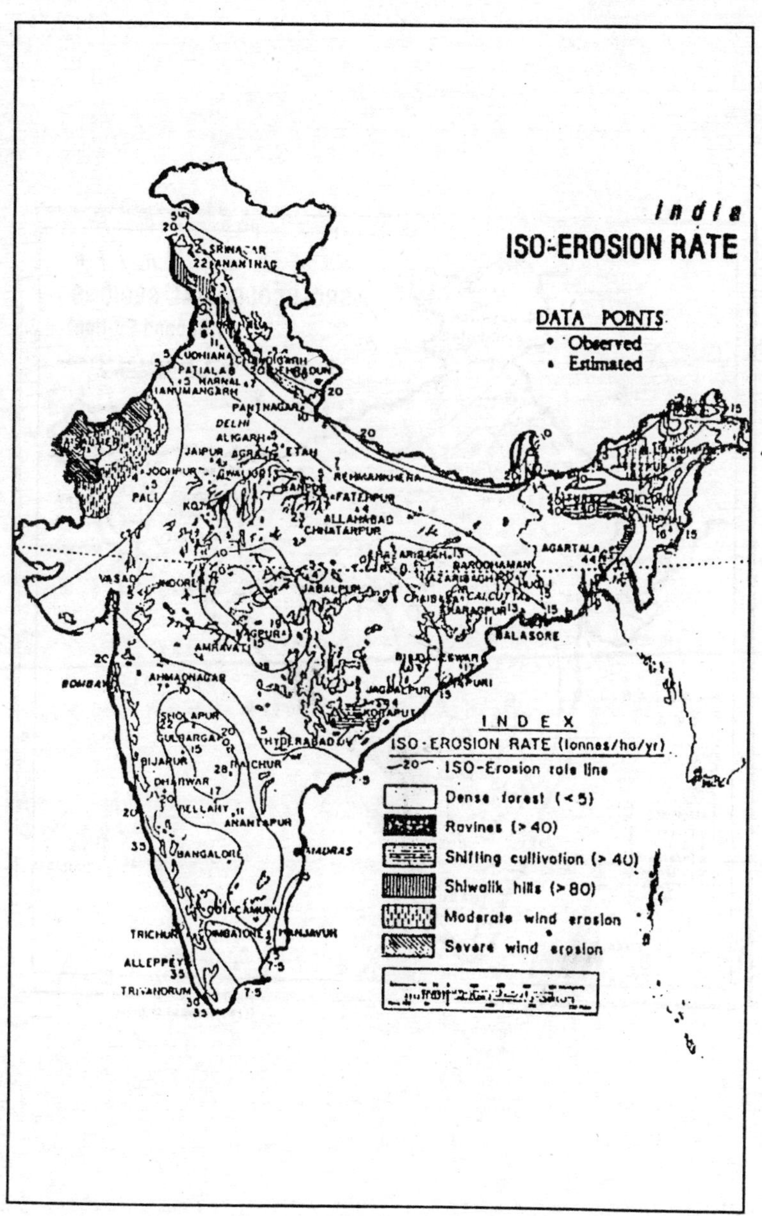
India
ISO-EROSION RATE
DATA POINTS
• Observed
• Estimated
INDEX
ISO-EROSION RATE (tonnes/ha/yr)
20 ISO-Erosion rate line
Dense forest (< 5)
Ravines (> 40)
Shifting cultivation (> 40)
Shiwalik hills (> 80)
Moderate wind erosion
Severe wind erosion
SRINAGAR
ANANTNAG
LUDHIANA
PATIALA
KARNAL
PANTNAGAR
DELHI
ALIGARH
ETAH
JAIPUR
AGRA
JODHPUR
PALI
KOTA
FATEHPUR
ALLAHABAD
CHHATARPUR
AGARTALA
SHILLONG
HAZARIBAGH
CALCUTTA
KHARAGPUR
BALASORE
JABALPUR
INDORE
VASAD
NAGPUR
AMRAVATI
BOMBAY
AHMADNAGAR
SHOLAPUR
GULBARGA
BIJAPUR
RAICHUR
HYDERABAD
JAGDALPUR
KORAPUT
DHARWAR
BELLARY
ANANTAPUR
BANGALORE
MADRAS
OOTACAMUND
COIMBATORE
THANJAVUR
TRICHUR
ALLEPPEY
TRIVANDRUM

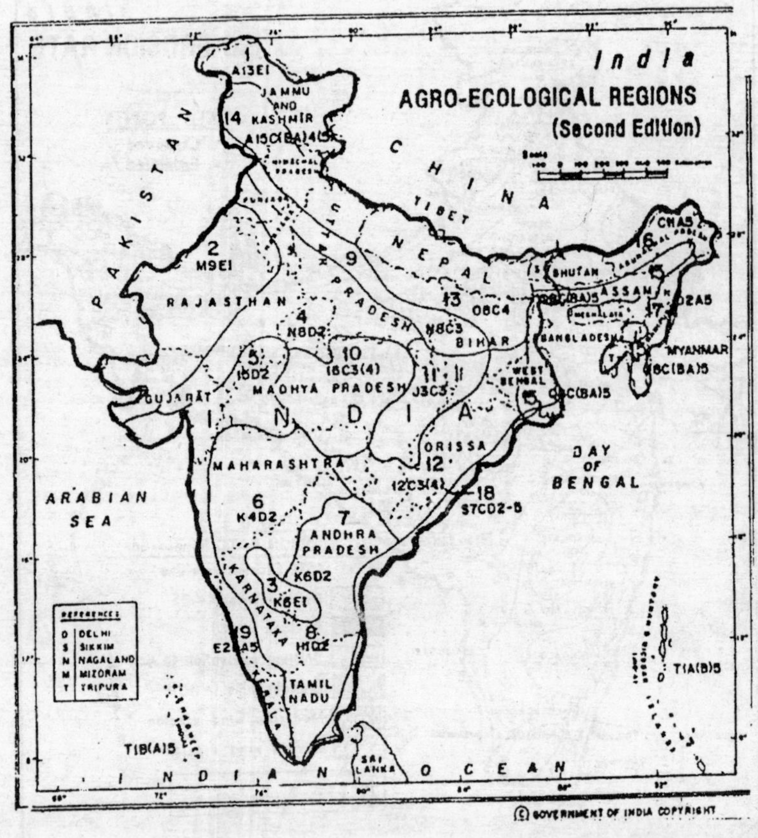
India
AGRO-ECOLOGICAL REGIONS
(Second Edition)
PAKISTAN
CHINA
TIBET
NEPAL
BHUTAN
ASSAM
BANGLADESH
MYANMAR
JAMMU AND KASHMIR
RAJASTHAN
UTTAR PRADESH
BIHAR
MADHYA PRADESH
GUJARAT
INDIA
WEST BENGAL
ORISSA
MAHARASHTRA
ANDHRA PRADESH
KARNATAKA
TAMIL NADU
KERALA
SRI LANKA
ARABIAN SEA
BAY OF BENGAL
INDIAN OCEAN
REFERENCES
D DELHI
S SIKKIM
N NAGALAND
M MIZORAM
T TRIPURA
1 A13E1
2 M9E1
3 K6E1
4 N8D2
5 I5D2
6 K4D2
7 K6D2
8 H1D2
9
10 I6C3(4)
11 J3C3
12 12C3(4)
13 O8C4
14 A15C(BA)4(5)
18 S7CD2-5
19 E2A5
T1B(A)5
T1A(B)5
© GOVERNMENT OF INDIA COPYRIGHT

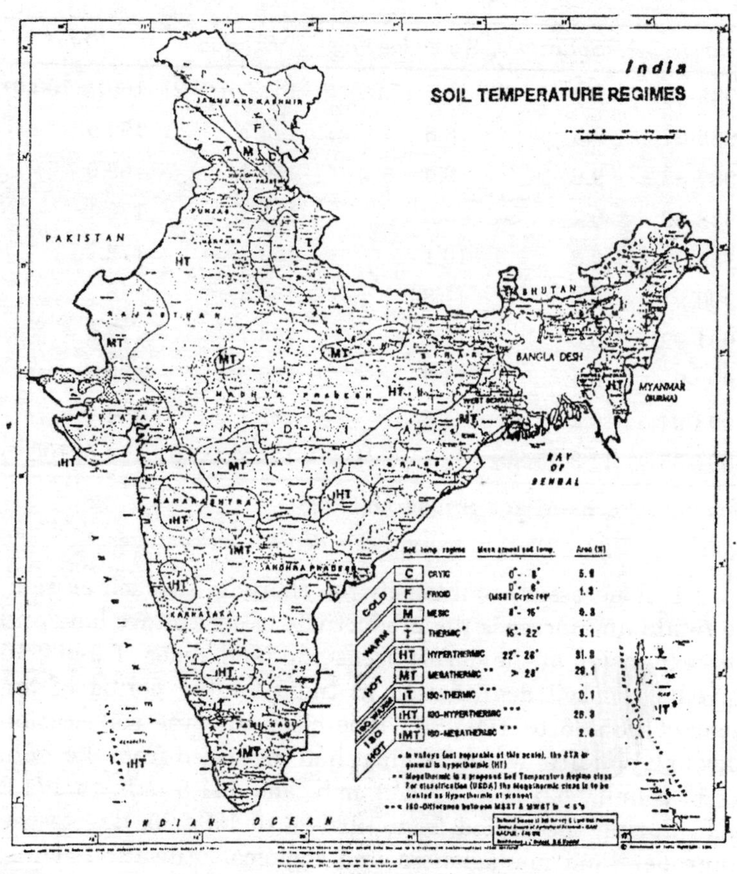
India
SOIL TEMPERATURE REGIMES
JAMMU AND KASHMIR
PAKISTAN
PUNJAB
BHUTAN
BANGLA DESH
MYANMAR (BURMA)
RAJASTHAN
MADHYA PRADESH
BIHAR
WEST BENGAL
GUJARAT
INDIA
ORISSA
MAHARASHTRA
ANDHRA PRADESH
KARNATAKA
TAMIL NADU
BAY OF BENGAL
INDIAN OCEAN
COLD
WARM
HOT
ISO WARM
ISO HOT
C CRYIC
F FRIGID
M MESIC
T THERMIC
HT HYPERTHERMIC 22°- 28° 31.8
MT MEGATHERMIC ** > 28° 29.1
iT ISO-THERMIC *** 0.1
iHT ISO-HYPERTHERMIC *** 28.3
iMT ISO-MEGATHERMIC *** 2.8

fertilizer-N as ammonia gas is called ammonia volatilization. The presence of ammonia and sulfur dioxide may lead to acid rains ultimately degrade the soil. Atmospheric ammonia contaminate water bodies, impairs visibility and causes corrosion. Nitrous oxide also contributes to global warming.

Table 2.9: Soil Degradation in India (in Million hectare)

Year	*Solidity*	*Water logging*	*Erosion*	*Total*
1985-86	9.4 (5.86)	8.5 (5.29)	141.5 (58.2)	160.4 (100.0)
1986-87	9.5	8.8	143.7	162.0
1987-88	9.6	9.0	150.4	169.0
1988-89	9.7	9.2	151.2	170.1
1989-90	9.8	10.1	152.8	172.7
1990-91	9.9	11.8	154.5	176.2
1991-92	10.0	11.2	156.7	177.9
1992-93	10.1	11.3	159.3	180.7
1993-94	10.2	11.6	162.4	194.1
1994-95	11.3 (5.80)	12.1 (6.21)	171.2 (87.9)	194.6 (100.0)

Source: Pachauri and Sridharan (1998).

Note: Figures within parenthesis denotes percentages.

It is necessary to intensify the efforts to stop soil erosion, to retain and increase the productivity of agriculture land and the expansion of the desert areas and land slides. Table 2.10 reveals the soil degradation in India for the period of ten years (1985-86 to 1994-95). It is clear that the soil erosion through solidity, water lagging, had increased from 9.4 m.h. to 11.3 m.h., 8.5 m.h. to 12.1 m.h. and 141.5 m.h. to 171.2 m.h. during the period from 1985-86 to 1994-95, due to the improper land management and chemical utilisation. Thus, the soil degradation had increased from 160 m.h. to 194.5 m.h. in India during the period from 1985-86 to 1994-95.

Area under Irrigation

Water requirements of crop depend primarily on climate and soil factors. Crop season in India is predominately Kharif

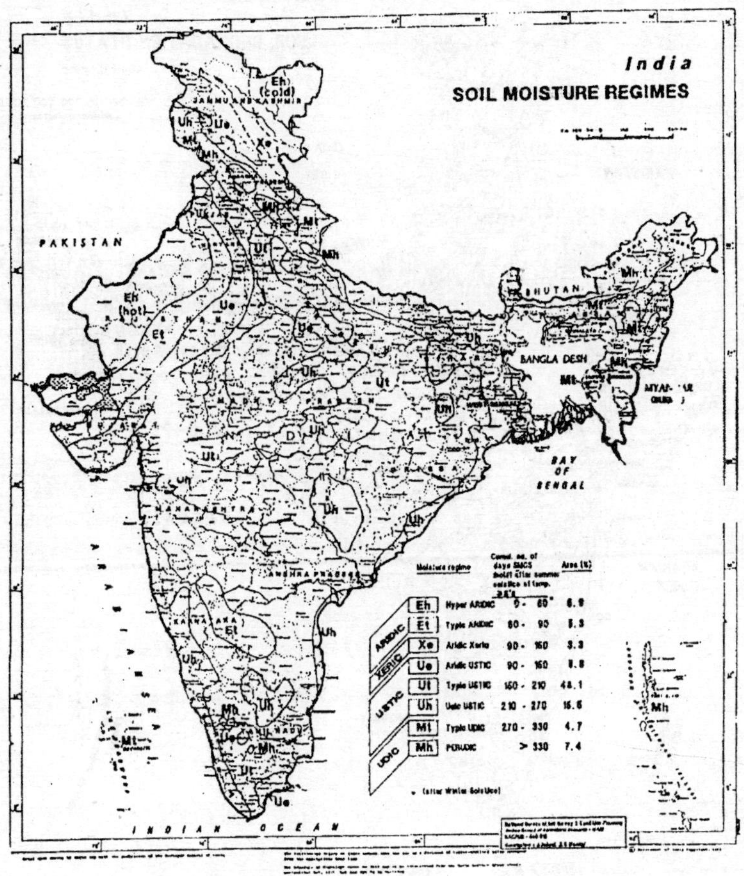
India
SOIL MOISTURE REGIMES
PAKISTAN
JAMMU AND KASHMIR
Eh (cold)
Eh (hot)
RAJASTHAN
MADHYA PRADESH
MAHARASHTRA
ANDHRA PRADESH
KARNATAKA
TAMIL NADU
ORISSA
BHUTAN
BANGLA DESH
BAY OF BENGAL
INDIAN OCEAN
Moisture regime
Area (%)
Eh Hyper ARIDIC 9 - 60*
Et Typic ARIDIC 60 - 90
Xe Aridic Xeric 90 - 160 3.3
Ue Aridic USTIC 90 - 160
Ut Typic USTIC 160 - 210 48.1
Uh Udic USTIC 210 - 270
Mt Typic UDIC 270 - 330 4.7
Mh PERUDIC > 330 7.4
ARIDIC
XERIC
USTIC
UDIC

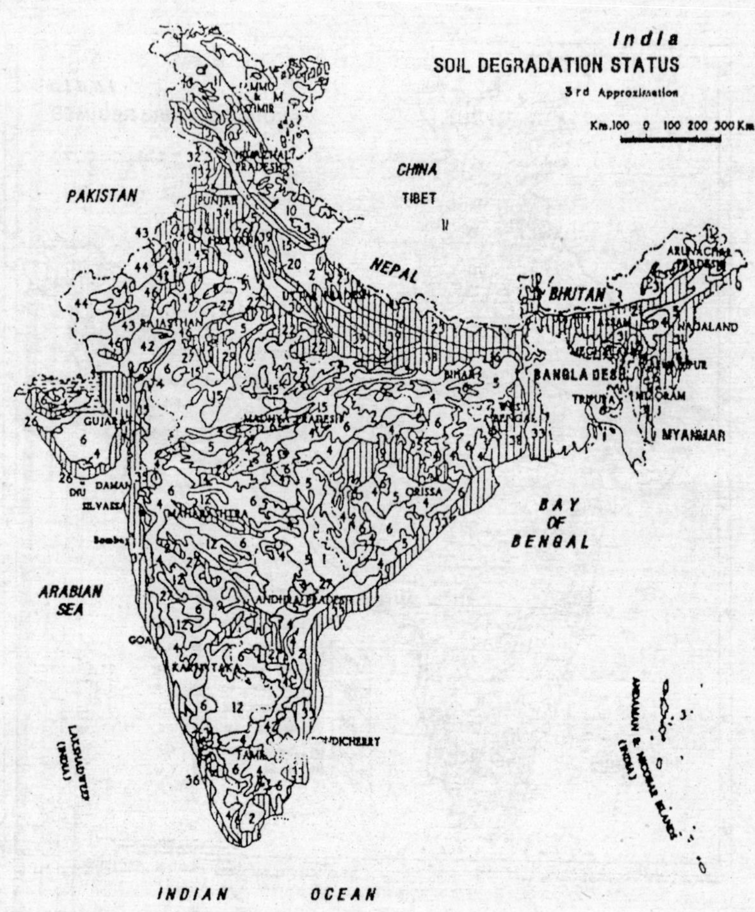
India
SOIL DEGRADATION STATUS
3rd Approximation
Km.100 0 100 200 300 Km
PAKISTAN
CHINA
TIBET
NEPAL
BHUTAN
BANGLA DESH
MYANMAR
BAY OF BENGAL
ARABIAN SEA
INDIAN OCEAN
PUNJAB
RAJASTHAN
GUJARAT
MADHYA PRADESH
MAHARASHTRA
ORISSA
ANDHRA PRADESH
KARNATAKA
ASSAM
NAGALAND
MIZORAM
TRIPURA
ARUNACHAL PRADESH
DAMAN
DIU
SILVASSA
Bombay
GOA
POUDICHERRY

followed by rabi. The area under cultivation during hot weather is very small being less than 5 per cent. During Kharif, the monsoon meets a substantial part of water requirements of crops, within limits some extra moisture stress does not seriously affect yield. Deep rooted crop can tolerate longer dry spells than the shallow rooted ones similarly, hot weather crops use up water at a faster rate than Rabi and Kharif crops because of the higher rate of evapo-transpiration in summer.

Different crops require different quantities of water supply throughout their growing period. The total water requirements of crops varies from 10.6 acre inches for mustard to 95.0 acre-inches for sugarcane. The water needs of other crops are linseed 12.7 acre-inches, hardly 14.1 outs 14.4 wheat 14.8; maize 17.8; jawar 25.7; groundnut 26.1 potato 26.7; ragi 29.8; chilies 28.8; tobacco 29.2; rice 41.7 and cotton 42.2 acre inches. The ICAR Hand book gives the water requirements of some major crops as below:

Table 2.10: Water Requirements of Major Crops in India

Crop	*Growing Season (days)*	*Total Water requirements (acre-inches)*	*Daily Water requirements (acre-inches)*
Rice	98	41.7	0.43
Wheat	88	14.8	0.17
Sugarcane	365	95.0	0.26
Cotton	202	42.2	0.11
Groundnut	124	26.1	0.21
Jawar	114	25.1	0.23
Potato	88	26.7	0.30

Source: Ministry of Agriculture and Cooperation, New Delhi-1997.

In addition to the above crops, the water requirements of deciduous fruit trees is about 30 inches, and of citrus and evergreen trees, about 40 inches a year. Touch crops such as

River basins : Water stress and water scarcity

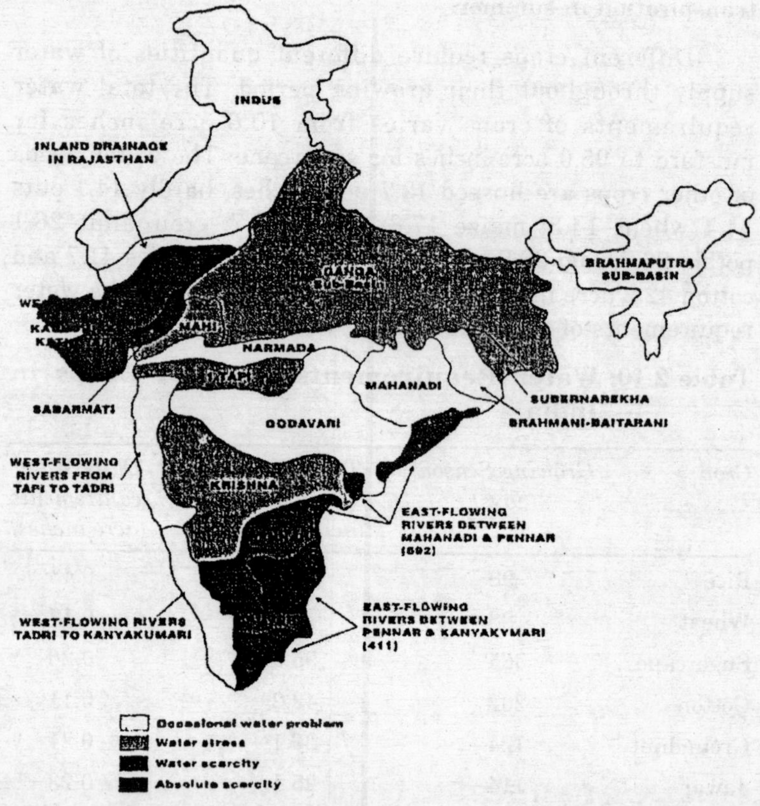

beans, lettuce and water melons require about 16 inches of water, common feeder grasses about 24 inches and perennial legumes such as Lucerne, berseem and clover about 36 inches of water per year. When the required quantity is not available through natural water supply, irrigation has to be restored to.

Whenever rain fails, i.e., when it is less than 80 per cent of the average, or when it does not occur at the proper crop seasons, production falls. If deficiency of rainfall is 40 per cent or more, famines result and crop do not evergreen. In order to banish famines the only source is artificial supply of water to the lands through irrigation. Some Canal Command Area and the Krishna and Godawari deltas, which are today the granaries of rice, used to be famine-ridden only a few years back. Irrigation is the antidote to famine.

Ground water sources contributed nearly 51% of the total area irrigated in 1991-92. There has been a drastic increase in the utilization of ground water resources setting depleted, surface water sources, rivers, canals, tanks and have also been affected considerably due to the degradation and situation of riverbeds.

In India, the growing population demands higher quantities of foodgrains for its consumption but in the absence of which imports ranging from Rs. 150 to Rs. 200 crores per annum have to be made to cut short imports and self sufficiency in food grains is very necessary. This can be achieved besides putting various inputs in the fields, through increasing area under cultivation and the yield of crops, the first place must be given to the works for the supply and conservation of water.

The net area under irrigation has increased from 41.86 mha in 1985-86 to 53.00 mha in 1994-95. (Table 2.11). The development in irrigation potential is largely due to the efforts of the Government in developing irrigation facilities through major/medium and minor irrigation projects.

Table 2.11: Area Irrigated in India (m.ha)

Years	*Net Area Irrigated*	*Gross Irrigated Area*
1985-86	41.86 (12.72)	54.28
1986-87	42.73 (12.98)	55.11
1987-88	43.01 (13.07)	57.64
1988-89	44.27 (13.45)	59.83
1989-90	45.55 (13.84)	60.17
1990-91	47.78 (14.52)	62.47
1991-92	49.87 (15.15)	65.68
1992-93	50.37 (15.31)	66.76
1993-94	51.34 (15.60)	68.25
1994-95	53.00 (16.10)	70.65

Source: Department of Agriculture & Co-operation, Ministry of Agriculture New Delhi 1994.

Note: Figures with in parenthesis denotes percentages.

Table 2.12: Area Under Irrigated Crops in India (crop wise)

Crops	*1985-86*	*86-87*	*87-88*	*88-89*	*89-90*
Rice	41.3	41.3	41.88	41.9	42.5
Wheat	22.1	22.6	22.9	23.2	23.5
Pulses	22.6	23.3	24.1	24.3	24.6
Food grains	126.8	127.3	127.6	126.7	127.7
Cotton	7.3	7.1	7.5	7.6	7.5
Jute	1.3	1.2	1.3	1.1	1.2
Sugarcane	2.8	2.9	3.1	3.2	3.6
Tabacco	0.6	0.8	0.5	0.3	0.4
Oil	17.7	17.5	18.6	21.3	22.2

Source: Ministry of Agriculture & Cooperation, New Delhi 1999.

At present 20 per cent of the cropped area of the country in under cash crops, which produces 30 per cent of the country's production commanding 33.3 per cent of the total

Table 2.13: Area Irrigated Crops in India

Crops	*90-91*	*91-92*	*92-93*	*93-94*	*94-95*
Rice	42.7	42.6	42.5	42.3	42.2
Wheat	24.2	24.6	24.3	25.5	25.6
Pulses	24.7	25.1	25.3	24.0	23.2
Food	127.8	127.1	126.4	124.2	123.5
Grains cotton	7.4	7.6	7.7	7.7	7.9
Jute	1.0	1.1	1.2	0.8	0.9
Sugarcane	3.7	3.6	3.5	3.7	3.8
Tobacco	0.4	0.4	0.4	0.4	0.4
Oil	24.1	24.2	24.8	24.3	25.3

Source: Ministry of Agriculture, Cooperation, New Delhi 1999.

value of agricultural products. Only about 12 per cent area under cash crop is irrigated at present. As it is known cash crops ensure employment through industries, and about 60 per cent of the annual foreign exchange earnings come from these products (pepper, spices, tobacco, cashew nuts, cotton, jute and oil seeds etc.). Therefore their productivity can be stepped up through provision of increased irrigation facilities with regard to cereals, where the mean percentage variation in production from year to year is large, improvement in irrigation facilities leads to higher yields.

While about 46.8 per cent of the net area shown during 1994-95 while lands under cultivable waste have been steadily declining from 5.1 per cent in 1985-86 to 4.7 per cent in 1994-95.

Cropping Intensity

The cropping intensity in India is explained in table 2.15. The cropping intensity has raised from 126.55 million hectare to 131.50 million hectare during the study period from 1985-86 to 1994-95. Besides, there was hardly any difference in intensity of cropping in irrigated and unirrigated areas. The cropping intensity of agriculture was low (115 to 118 p.c.) as compared to that in similar condition in other countries.

Table 2.14: Net Area Sown in India

Year	Net area sown in (m.ha)	% of net area sown	Gross sown area (in m.h.)	% of more than as % of net area sown
1985-86	146.13	45.8	184.34	26.7
1986-87	147.66	43.9	183.92	26.4
1987-88	148.42	46.5	185.61	27.3
1988-89	140.10	46.4	184.33	28.5
1989-90	140.00	46.6	183.28	28.1
1990-91	143.00	46.3	185.74	30.7
1991-92	140.61	46.7	182.24	29.2
1992-93	185.70	46.7	185.62	30.2
1993-94	142.42	46.7	186.00	31.0
1994-95	142.96	46.8	188.05	31.7

Source: Department of Agriculture and Co-operation, Ministry of Agriculture, New Delhi 1999.

Table 2.15: Cropping Intensity in India (in mha)

Year	Cropping Intensity	Year	Cropping Intensity
1985-86	126.55 (38.46)	1990-91	129.90 (39.48)
1986-87	127.47 (38.74)	1991-92	128.70 (39.11)
1987-88	128.12 (39.94)	1992-93	130.10 (39.54)
1988-89	128.53 (39.06)	1993-94	131.02 (39.82)
1989-90	129.88 (39.47)	1994-95	131.50 (39.96)

Source: Department of Agriculture and Co-operation, Ministry of Agriculture, New Delhi 1997.

Note: Figures with in parenthesis denotes percentages.

Agricultural Yield

The Tables 2.16 and 2.17 reveal the yield rate of crops in India during the period from 1985-86 to 1994-94. It is clear that the yield rate for all crops except jowar, maize, bajra had increased during the study period Rice yield rate had increased from 1274 to 1911, and for maize rate had decreased from 2420 to 1448 during the period from 1985-86 to 1994-95.

Table 2.16: Yield Rate of Crops in India

Crop	*1985-86*	*86-87*	*87-88*	*88-89*	*89-90*
Rice	1274	1385	1392	1442	1511
Wheat	2011	2181	1941	2010	2055
Jowar	1417	1380	1305	1300	1212
Maize	2420	2285	2213	2012	1934
Bajra	580	613	720	672	945
Potato	9000	12000	10000	11000	14000
Groundnut	847	980	1160	1280	1315
Cotton	200	210	266	195	230
Sugarcane	50000	52000	55000	58000	59000

Source: Economic Survey, Ministry of Finance, GOI, New Delhi, 1997-98.

Table 2.17: Yield Rate of Crops in India

Crop	*1990-91*	*91-92*	*92-93*	*93-94*	*94-95*
Rice	1601	1619	1744	1888	1911
Wheat	2143	2241	2327	2380	2559
Jowar	1167	1012	982	898	779
Maize	1875	1753	1676	1602	1448
Bajra	810	745	836	521	700
Potato	13000	15000	14000	17000	16000
Groundnut	1426	1612	1049	941	1027
Cotton	274	261	257	249	257
Sugarcane	61000	63000	64000	67000	71000

Source: Economic Survey, Ministry of Finance, GOI, New Delhi, 1997-98.

Table 2.18: Performance of Crop Production in India (in M.h.)

Year	*1985-86*	*86-87*	*87-88*	*88-89*	*89-90*
Rice	63.84	64.33	72.55	68.24	71.16
Wheat	48.17	49.51	53.64	50.84	51.83
Coarse Cereals	21.66	21.78	24.55	23.13	24.66
Total cereals	127.45	131.06	130.12	125.66	137.5
Total pulses	11.22	11.18	10.95	11.80	11.06
Total foodgrains	120.61	128.75	138.33	150.66	143.10
Sugarcane	121.88	110.5	112.85	236.73	241.88
Total Oil Seeds	10.46	10.11	11.66	13.55	14.51
Cotton@	14.31	9.76	10.88	9.83	8.53
Jute & Musta	10.55	11.66	11.89	9.10	9.41
Non food Grains	110.17	120.92	125.88	126.72	135.11

Source: Agricultural Statistics at a Glance, 1998.

@: Production in Million bales 170 kg earn # : Production in Million bales 180 kg earn * : Index number Page: 1981-82.

Tables 2.18 and 2.19 reveal the performance of crop production in India. It is clear that the total foodgrains production level was increased from 120.61 m.h. in 1985-86 to 191.50 m.h. in 1994-95. Similarly the total non foodgrains production also increased from 110.17 to 180.90 mh during the same period.

It is estimated that the production of total foodgrains increased at a rate of 6% and that rice and pulses at the rate of 10% and 20% respectively in the sub region. The growth rate of foodgrains production varied depend upon the level of irrigation, use of agricultural inputs and prevailing climate condition during the reported agricultural season.

Table 2.19: Performance of Crop Production in India (in M.h.)

Year	*90-91*	*91-92*	*92-93*	*93-94*	*94-95*
Rice	75.32	74.68	72.86	80.30	81.81
Wheat	53.68	55.69	57.2	59.84	65.77
Coarse cereals	25.53	25.99	36.59	30.82	29.88
Total cereals	157.62	156.36	166.67	170.96	177.46
Total Pulses	12.10	12.02	12.82	13.30	14.04
Total foodgrains	164.33	168.38	179.48	184.26	191.50
Sugarcane	249.2	254.00	228.03	229.66	275.54
Total Oil Seeds	17.57	18.60	20.11	21.50	21.34
Cotton @	9.66	9.71	11.40	10.74	11.89
Jute & Musta#	9.85	10.29	8.59	8.43	9.08
Noon food Grains	140.55	158.80	164.00	169.50	180.90

Source: Agricultural statistics at a glance. 1998.

@: Production in Million bales 170 kg earn # : Production in Million bales 180 kg earn*: Index number page: 1981-82

Utilisation of Fertilisers and Pesticides

The present coverage of green manuring is estimated at 7m hectares about 5.8 m tonnes of urban compost was available in 1977-78 as against 5.4 m tonnes in 1976-77. Under the Fifth Five Year Plan, the targets of fertilisers consumption have been placed at 5200 thousand tonnes of N; 1800 thousand tonnes of P2 O5 and that of K2O at 1000 thousand tones. The consumption of fertilisers has been continuously increasing from 21.8 lakh tonnes in 1970-71 to about 91 lakh tonnes in 1987-88. Consumption of phosphoric and potassic fertilisers is also increasing continuously in the post green revolution periods.

The Table 2.20 shows the consumption of fertilisers in India during the period from 1985-86 to 1994-95. The use of Nitrogen are higher than the (36.8 lakhs tonnes) phosphate and potassic (12.1 lakhs tonnes and 6.2 lakhs tonnes) in 1985-86. It implies that the total use of Nitrogen, Potassic had increased from 55.2 lakhs million tonnes to 115.1 lakhs tonnes during the study period.

Table 2.20: Consumption of Fertilizers (in Lakhs tonnes)

Year	*Nitrogen*	*Phosphatic*	*Potassic*	*Total*
1985-86	36.8 (66.8)	12.1 (21.9)	6.2 (11.3)	55.2 (100.0)
1986-87	54.9	18.9	8.4	82.1
1987-88	58.2	20.7	8.5	87.4
1988-89	59.3	22.6	9.2	91.1
1989-90	62.1	24.3	10.5	96.6
1990-91	63.3	26.2	11.3	100.8
1991-92	64.5	28.1	11.6	104.2
1992-93	67.6	29.5	12.8	109.9
1993-94	68.1	30.1	13.4	111.6
1994-95	69.6 (60.4)	30.8 (26.8)	14.7 (12.8)	115.1 (100.0)

Source: Ministry of Agriculture and Cooperation, New Delhi 1999.

Note: Figures within parenthesis denotes percentages.

Environmental Degradation in Tamil Nadu

This section analysed the environment degradation in Tamil Nadu by using the secondary data regarding the land use pattern, irrigation, cropping pattern, production level, consumption of fertilizers and pesticides for the period of ten years.

Net Area Sown

The net area sown in Tamil Nadu state during the study period is given in Table 2.21.

Table 2.22 reveals that while about 40 per cent of the state geographical area is under the net area sown in 1985-86, it has increased from 51.6 lakhs Hectares to 57.9 lakhs hectares in 1994-95. However in Tamil Nadu, area under net area sown was increased in 6.3 lakhs hectares during the period from 1985-86 to 1994-95. The percentage to the total geographical area in net area sown has been increased from 39.63 per cent in 1985-86 to 44.7 per cent in 1994-95.

TAMIL NADU
FOREST MA
BAY OF BENGAL
VIRUDHU NAGAR
TIRUNELVELI
TUTICORIN
GULF OF
MANNAR
FOREST
AREA.

Table 2.21: Net Area Sown in Tamil Nadu (in Hec)

Year	Net sown area	Year	Net sown area
1985-86	51.6 (39.63)	1990-91	55.8 (42.85)
1986-87	55.7 (42.78)	1991-92	57.3 (44.00)
1987-88	52.2 (40.09)	1992-93	58.1(44.62)
1988-89	51.4 (39.47)	1993-94	59.0 (45.31)
1989-90	54.3 (41.70)	1994-95	57.9 (44.47)

Source: Agro statistics, Directorate of Agriculture 1996.

Note: Figures within parenthesis denotes percentage to Geographical area.

Fallow Lands

Net sown area and fallow lands together constitute agriculture land, which may also be termed as cultivated land. In 1980-81 out of the total reporting area of 21.06 lakh hectare of the sub-region, about 4.5% were reported as wet area sown, which was comparable to 41.22% in the state. The current fallow lands in Tamil Nadu is given in Table 2.22.

Table 2.22: Current Fallow lands in Tamil Nadu (in lakhs Hectare)

Year	Fallow Lands		Geographical areas
1985-86	11.82	(9.07)	130.0
1986-87	13.83	(10.62)	130.1
1987-88	9.45	(7.25)	130.2
1988-89	10.36	(7.95)	130.0
1989-90	11.04	(8.47)	130.1
1990-91	12.7	(9.75)	130.2
1991-92	10.6	(8.14)	130.2
1992-93	9.6	(7.37)	130.1
1993-94	9.3	(7.14)	130.2
1994-95	10.0	(7.68)	130.0

Source: Agro Statistics, Directorate of Agriculture, Chennai. 1996.

Note: Figures with in parenthesis denotes percentage of current fallow land to total geographical area.

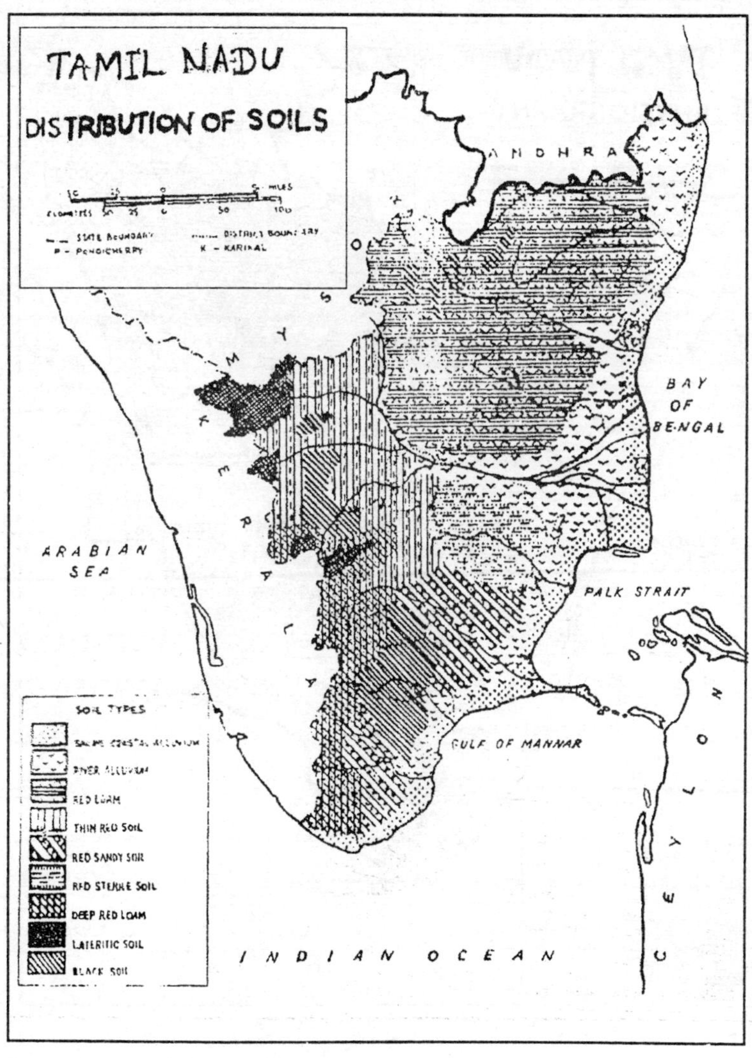
TAMIL NADU
DISTRIBUTION OF SOILS
MILES
K - KARIKAL
ANDHRA
BAY OF BENGAL
ARABIAN SEA
PALK STRAIT
GULF OF MANNAR
INDIAN OCEAN
CEYLON
KERALA
SOIL TYPES
RED LOAM
THIN RED SOIL
RED SANDY SOIL
DEEP RED LOAM
LATERITIC SOIL

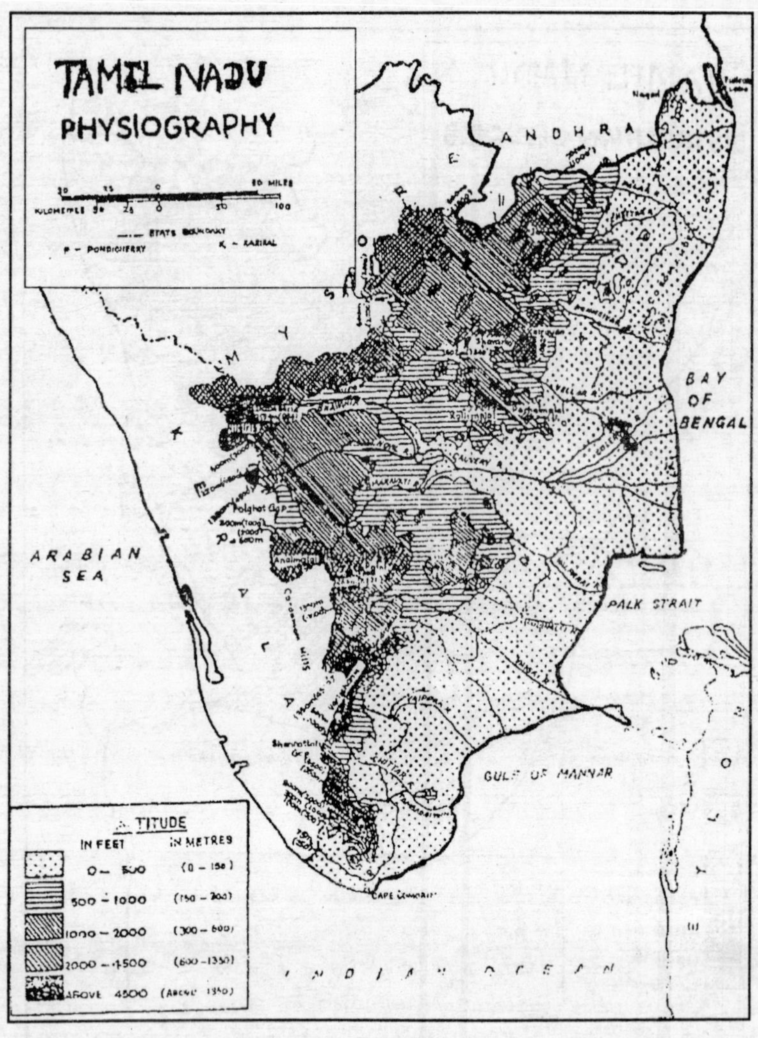
TAMIL NADU
PHYSIOGRAPHY
STATE BOUNDARY
P – PONDICHERRY
K – KARIKAL
ANDHRA
BAY OF BENGAL
ARABIAN SEA
PALK STRAIT
GULF OF MANNAR
INDIAN OCEAN
Palghat Gap
CAPE COMORIN
ALTITUDE
IN FEET
IN METRES
0 – 500
(0 – 150)
500 – 1000
(150 – 300)
1000 – 2000
(300 – 600)
2000 – 4500
(600 – 1350)
ABOVE 4500
(ABOVE 1350)

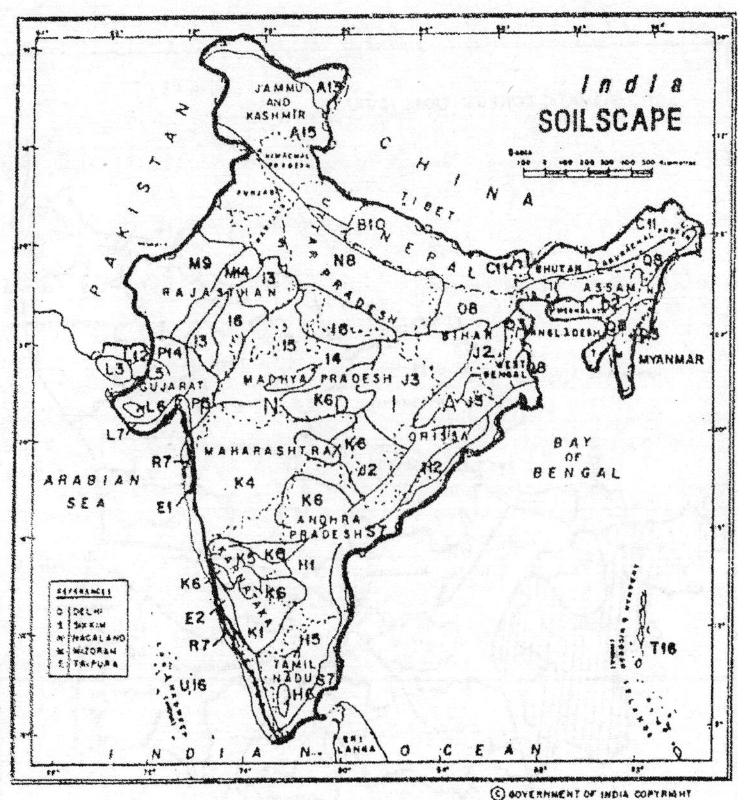

Key (for decoding)

PHYSIOGRAPHY (1st Letter)

(A) Western Himalayas, (B) Central Himalayas, (C) Eastern Himalayas, (D) North-Eastern Hills, (E) Western Ghats, (H) Eastern Ghats, (I) Central Highland, (J) Eastern Plateau, (K) Deccan Plateau, (L) Kachchh and Kathiawar Peninsula, (M) Western Plain, (N) Northern Plain, (O) Eastern Plain, (P) Gujarat Plain, (Q) Assam and Bengal Plain, (R) Western Coastal Plain, (S) Eatern Coastal Plain, (T) Eastern Islands, (U) Western Islands

SOILS (1st Number)

(1) Red Loamy Soils, (2) Red and Lateritic Soils, (3) Red and Yellow Soils, (4) Shallow and Medium-(inclusion Deep) Black Soils, (5) Medium and Deep Black Soils, (6) Mixed Red and Black Soils, (7) Coastal Alluvium-derived Soils, (8) Alluvium-derived Soils, (19) Desert (Saline) Soils. Z(10) Tarai Sopils, (11) Brown and Red Hill Soils, (12) Saline and Alkali Soils (observed in Patches in 5, 8, 11, 14, (13) Shallow Skeletal Soils, (14) Grey Brown Soils, (15) Brown Forest and Podzolic Soils, (16) Sandy and Littoral Soils

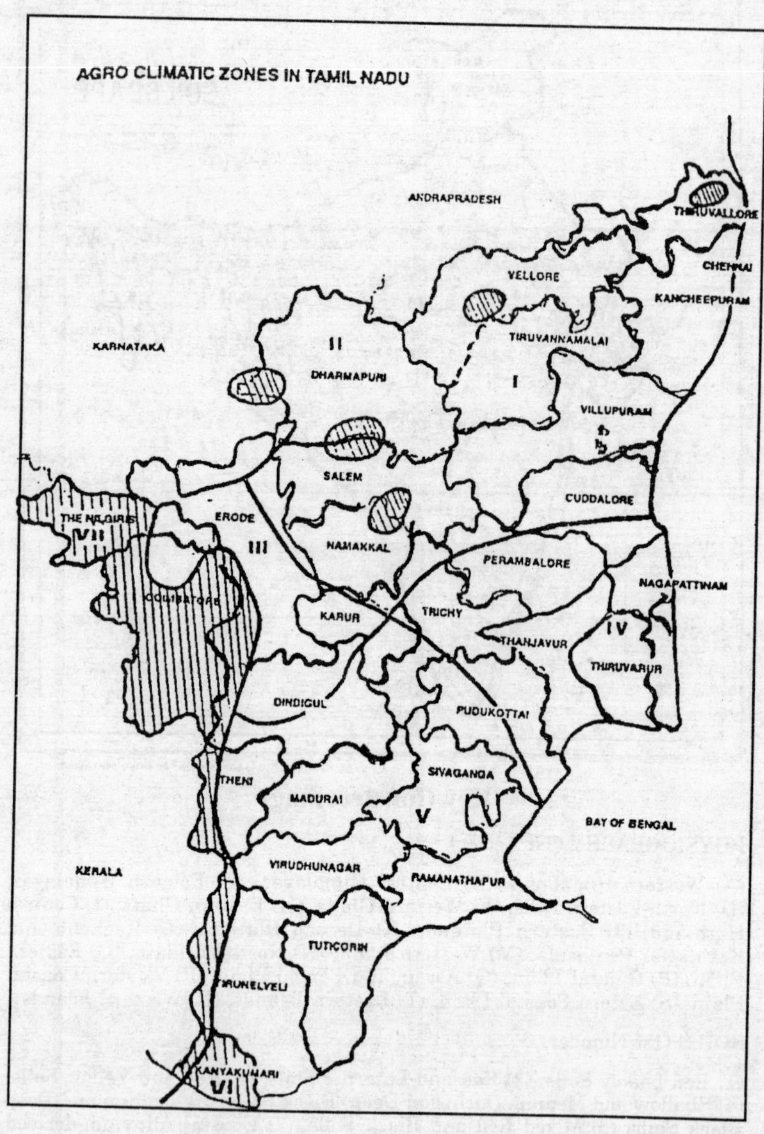
AGRO CLIMATIC ZONES IN TAMIL NADU
ANDRAPRADESH
THIRUVALLORE
CHENNAI
VELLORE
KANCHEEPURAM
KARNATAKA
II
DHARMAPURI
TIRUVANNAMALAI
I
VILLUPURAM
SALEM
CUDDALORE
THE NILGIRIS
VII
ERODE
III
NAMAKKAL
PERAMBALORE
NAGAPATTINAM
KARUR
TRICHY
THANJAVUR
IV
THIRUVARUR
DINDIGUL
PUDUKOTTAI
THENI
SIVAGANGA
MADURAI
V
BAY OF BENGAL
KERALA
VIRUDHUNAGAR
RAMANATHAPUR
TUTICORIN
TIRUNELVELI
KANYAKUMARI
VI

In 1985-86, out of the total reporting area of 130.0 lakhs hectares of the Tamil Nadu State, about 11.82 lakhs hectares is current fallow land which was comparable to 9.07 per cent of the geographical area. It has decreased to 10.0 lakhs hectatres in 1994-95 i.e. 7.6 per cent of the geographical area.

Cultivable and Uncultivable Waste Land

The cultivable waste land in Tamil Nadu is given in Table 2.23. The category cultivable wastes, permanent pastures and grazing lands and land under miscellaneous trade crops and groves.

Table 2.23: Cultivable waste land in Tamil Nadu (in lakhs hectares)

Year	*Cultivable Waste Land*	*Year*	*Cultivable Waste Land*
1985-86	4.1 (3.14)	1990-91	3.0 (2.30)
1986-87	3.8 (2.91)	1991-92	3.1 (2.38)
1987-88	3.7 (2.84)	1992-93	3.0 (2.30)
1988-89	3.1 (2.38)	1993-94	3.1 (2.38)
1889-90	2.2 (1.68)	1994-95	3.0 (2.30)

Source: Agro Statistics, Directorate of Agriculture, Chennai—1996.

Note: Figures within parenthesis denotes percentage of cultivable waste land to total geographical area.

Total area under this category of cultivable land was reported as 4.1 lakhs hectares in 1985-86 i.e. 3.14 percentage of the total geographical land. The proportion of cultivable waste land was declined to 3.0 lakh hectares which shows the 2.3 per cent of the total geographical area in Tamil Nadu.

Uncultivable land consists of land put to non-agricultural uses, barren and uncultivable land. About 4.0 per cent of the total area were under this category. Concentration of uncultivable land was same in the sub-regional average in Tamil Nadu. i.e., area under uncultivable land was 5 lakhs hectares in 1985-86 and in 1994-95.

Table 2.24: Uncultivable Lands in Tamil Nadu (in lakhs hectares)

Year	*Uncultivable Land*	*Year*	*Uncultivable Land*
1985-86	5.0 (3.84)	1990-91	5.1 (3.91)
1986-87	5.0 (3.84)	1991-92	5.1 (3.91)
1987-88	5.0 (3.84)	1992-93	5.1 (3.91)
1988-89	5.2 (3.99)	1993-94	5.2 (3.99)
1989-90	5.0 (3.84)	1994-95	5.0 (3.84)

Source: Agro state, Directorate of Agri-1996.

Note: Figures in Brackets indicate percentage to Geographical area.

Area under Irrigation

The source of irrigation to the principal crops for the different periods in Tamil Nadu is analysed in Table 2.25.

Table 2.25: Irrigated By Principal Crops in Tamil Nadu (in Lakhs hectare)

Source of irrigation	*1980-81*	*1990-91*	*1994-95*
Canal	8.89 (35.0)	7.69 (32.4)	8.44 (29.07)
Tanks	5.90 (22.0)	5.31 (22.3)	6.74 (23.23)
Wells	10.67 (42.0)	10.59 (44.6)	13.69 (47.16)
Other Sources	0.24 (1.0)	0.14 (0.7)	0.16 (0.55)
Total	25.70	23.73	29.03
Percentage % of net area irrigation sown	48.00	42.50	50.10
Gross area irrigated % of Gross area	32.04	28.94	35.88
Irrigated to total gross area sown	50.90	43.60	51.10
Intensity of Irrigation	128.20	122.00	123.59

Source: Agro Statistics, Directorate of Agriculture, Chennai. 1996.

Note: Figures within parenthesis indicate percentage of Geographical area.

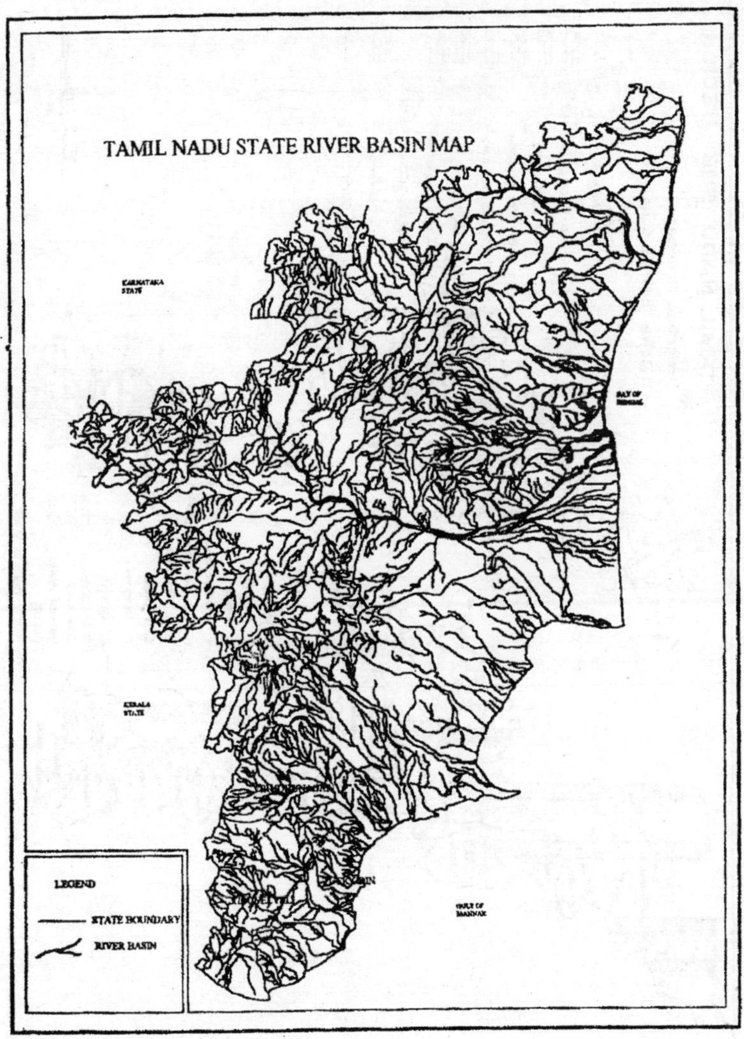
TAMIL NADU STATE RIVER BASIN MAP
KARNATAKA STATE
LEGEND
STATE BOUNDARY
RIVER BASIN

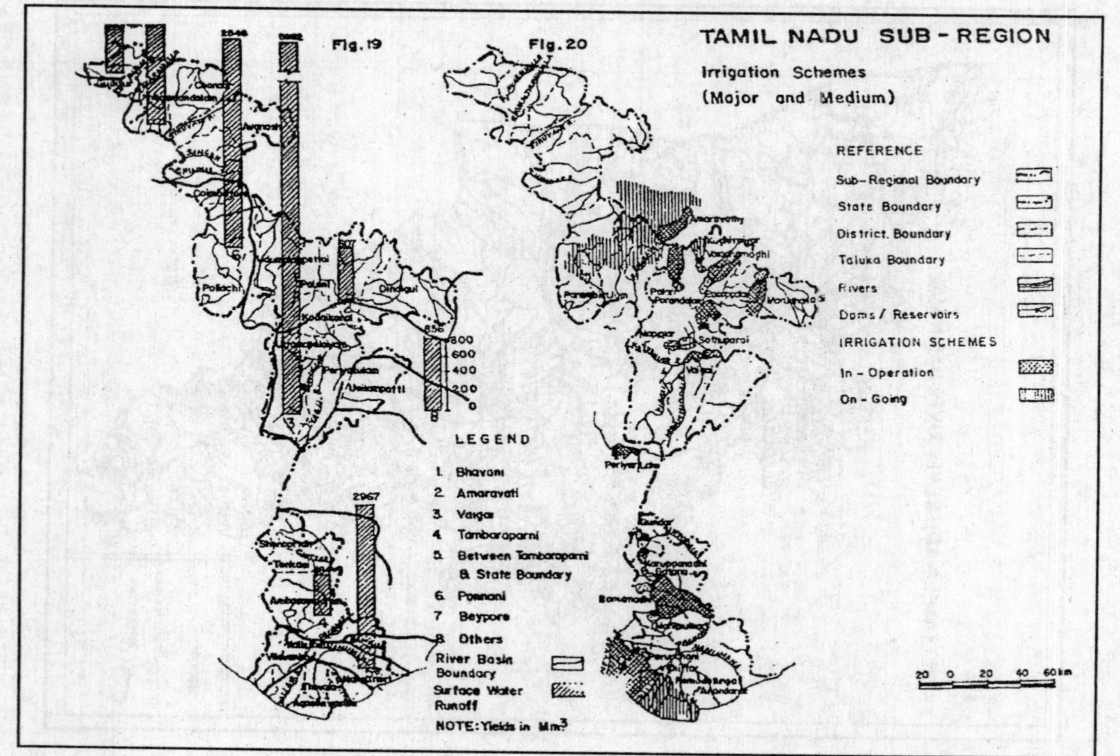
TAMIL NADU SUB-REGION
Irrigation Schemes
(Major and Medium)
Fig.19
Fig.20
REFERENCE
Sub-Regional Boundary
State Boundary
District Boundary
Taluka Boundary
Rivers
Dams / Reservoirs
IRRIGATION SCHEMES
In-Operation
On-Going
20 0 20 40 60 km
LEGEND
1. Bhavani
2. Amaravati
3. Vaigai
4. Tambaraparni
5. Between Tambaraparni & State Boundary
6. Ponnani
7. Beypore
8. Others
River Basin Boundary
Surface Water Runoff
NOTE: Yields in Mm3
800
600
400
200
0
856
2967
Pollachi
Palani
Dindigul
Kodaikanal
Periyakulam
Usilampatti
Amaravathy
Vaigai
Periyar Lake
Sothuparai

INDEX OF RIVER BASINS IN TAMILNADU

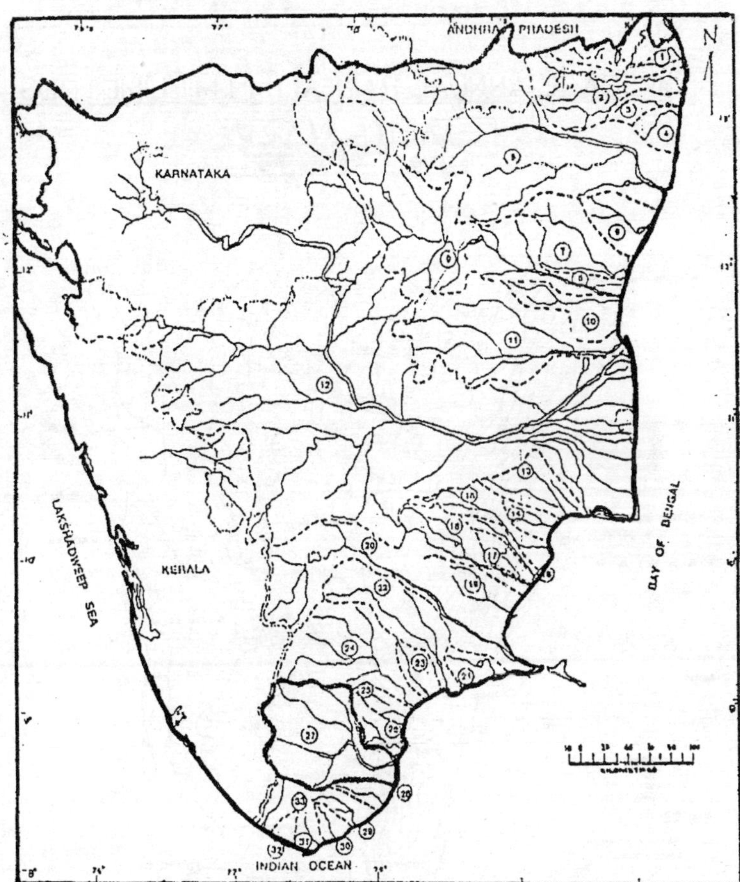

1. Araniyaru
2. Kortalaiyan
3. Cooum
4. Adayar
5. Palar
6. Ongurr
7. Varaha Nadhi
8. Nalattaru
9. Pennaiaru
10. Gadilam
11. Vellar
12. Cauvery
13. Agniaru
14. Amduliyaru
15. Vellar
16. Koluvanaru
17. Pamdar
18. Manimuthar
19. Kottakaraiaru
20. Vaigai
21. Uttarkosamangaiaru
22. Gundar
23. Vembaru
24. Vaipparu
25. Kallaru
26. Korampallamaru
27. Tambaraparani
28. Karamanaiaru
29. Namdyanu
30. Hanulia Nadhi
31. Palayaru
32. Valuar
33. Kodayar

WF. West Flowing

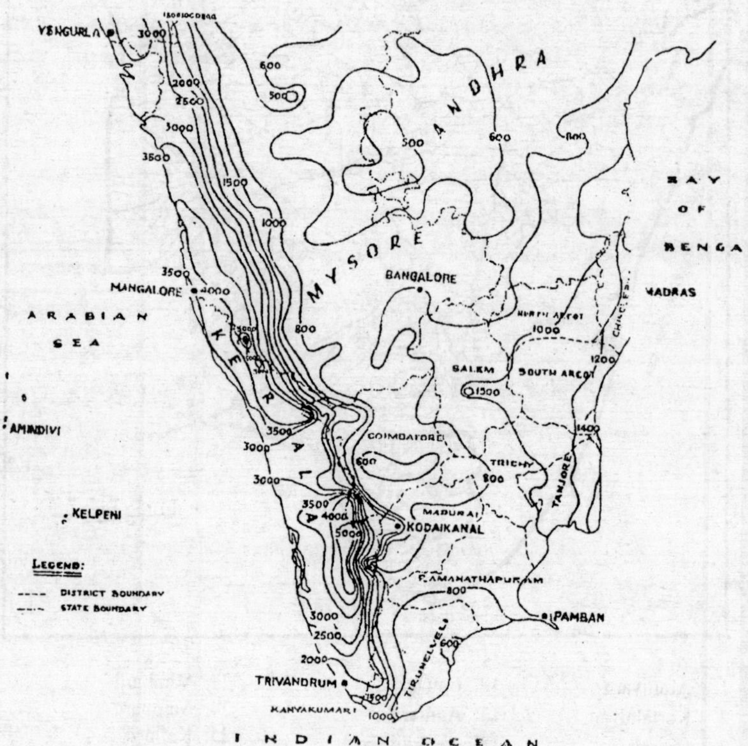
AVERAGE ANNUAL RAINFALL IN MILLIMETRES
TAMIL NADU
Scale:
VENGURLA
MYSORE
ANDHRA
KERALA
BANGALORE
MANGALORE
ARABIAN SEA
AMINDIVI
KELPENI
BAY OF BENGAL
MADRAS
NORTH ARCOT
SALEM
SOUTH ARCOT
COIMBATORE
TRICHY
TANJORE
MADURAI
KODAIKANAL
RAMANATHAPURAM
PAMBAN
TIRUNELVELI
TRIVANDRUM
KANYAKUMARI
INDIAN OCEAN
LEGEND:
DISTRICT BOUNDARY
STATE BOUNDARY

The percentage of area irrigated by canal has declined from 35 in 1980-81 to 29.07 in 1994-95. However there is undulating trend in case of area irrigated by tanks. Wells have shown a constant rise from 42 per cent in 1980-81 to 47.16 per cent in 1994-95 but the other sources has shown a constant downward trend. The total net area irrigated has shown an upward trend from 25.7 L. Ha in 1980-81 to 29.03 L.Ha in 1994-95 but with a fall (23.73 lakhs hectare) in 1990-91. An increasing trend is seen in case of net area irrigated with fall in 1990-91. The gross cropped area and cropping intensity were undulating over the years.

Table 2.26: Area Irrigated by Principal Crops in Tamil Nadu (Area in '000' Ha)

Crop	*1990-91*	*1991-92*	*1992-93*	*1993-94*	*1994-95*
Rice	1686 (43.29)	1968	2016	2137	2064 (57.52)
Cholam	46 (1.18)	38	37	42	39 (1.08)
Cumbu	29 (0.74)	23	20	19	23 (0.64)
Ragi	48 (1.97)	46	52	48	44 (1.22)
Maize	18 (0.46)	18	21	19	25 (0.69)
Sugarcane	233 (5.98)	238	216	248	328 (9.14)
Cotton	77 (1.97)	89	89	82	97 (2.70)
Groundnut	274 (7.03)	338	379	354	349 (9.69)
Other crops	483 (12.4)	509	555	594	620 (17.27)
Total Area Irrigated	3894(100.00)	3257	3885	3544	3588(100.00)

Source: Directorate of Statistics, Madras. 1999.

Note: Figures within parenthesis denotes percentages.

Cropped Area in Tamil Nadu

The total cropped area in Tamil Nadu for the study period is given in Table 2.27. It is clear from the table that the total cropped area has increased from 64.8 lakh hectares in 1985-86 to 70.3 lakhs hectare in 1994-95. The percentage of the total cropped area to the total geographical area has also increased from 49.76 in 1984-85 to 53.99 in 1994-95.

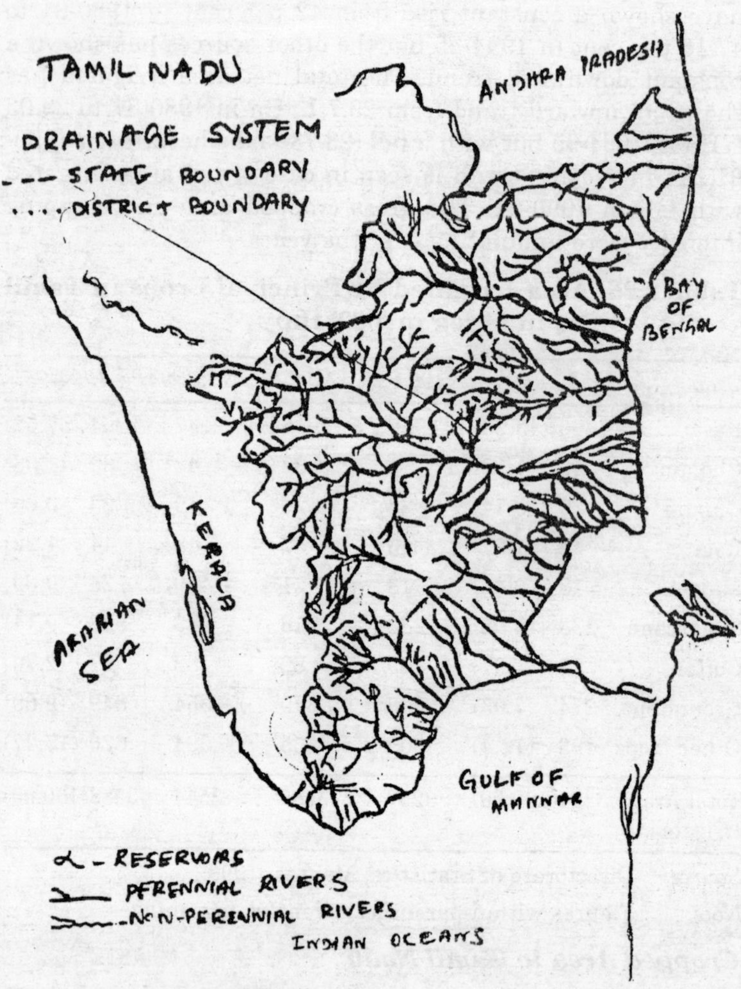
TAMIL NADU
DRAINAGE SYSTEM
--- STATE BOUNDARY
.... DISTRICT BOUNDARY
ANDHRA PRADESH
BAY OF BENGAL
KERALA
ARABIAN SEA
GULF OF MANNAR
RESERVOIRS
PERENNIAL RIVERS
NON-PERENNIAL RIVERS
INDIAN OCEANS

Table 2.27: Cropped Area in Tamil Nadu (in L.Ha)

Year	*Cropped Area*	*Year*	*Cropped Area*
1985-86	64.8 (49.76)	1990-91	66.3 (50.92)
1986-87	65.1 (50.00)	1991-92	69.8 (53.60)
1987-88	65.6 (50.38)	1992-93	70.6 (54.22)
1988-89	66.3 (50.92)	1993-94	71.6 (54.99)
1989-90	66.4 (50.99)	1994-95	70.3 (53.99)

Source: Agro statistics, Directorate of Agriculture—1996.

Note: Figures within parenthesis indicate percentage to total Geographical area.

Cropping Intensity

Degree of intensive cultivation is a fair index to assess the state of agricultural development. Position of intensity of cropping cultivation is better in the Tamil Nadu compared to other constituents of the western ghats region. The cropping intensity level is given in Table 2.28.

Table 2.28: Cropping Intensity in Tamil Nadu (in. L. Ha)

Year	*Cropping Intensity*	*Year*	*Cropping Intensity*
1985-86	121.4 (98.24)	1990-91	118.9 (91.32)
1986-87	117.3 (90.00)	1991-92	122.0 (93.70)
1987-88	115.5 (88.70)	1992-93	121.5 (93.31)
1988-89	119.1 (91.47)	1993-94	121.4 (93.24)
1989-90	121.9 (93.62)	1994-95	121.6 (93.39)

Source: Agro statistics, Directorate of Agriculture, 1996.

Note: Figures within parenthesis indicate percentage to total Geographical area.

The table 2.28 shows that the cropping intensity level is more or less same during the study period but the percentage has been decreased from 98.24 in 1985-86 to 93.39 in 1994-95. During 1985 86, intensity of cultivation in Tamil Nadu worked out to 121.4 lakhs hectare against 121.6 lakhs hectare in 1994-95 in the state. The higher degree of intensity of cultivation in the Tamil Nadu may be attributed to the light position of cultivated land which has also been reflected increases of intensity of cropping cultivation by 0.2 lakhs hectares during 1985-86 to 1994-95.

Cropping Pattern

The cropping pattern in Tamil Nadu is analysed in table 2.29 with the helps of the areas of major crops.

Table 2.29: Area of Major Crops in Tamil Nadu from (in Lakhs Hectares)

Year	*Rice*	*Cholam*	*Cumbu*	*Ragi*	*Maize*	*Other Millets*	*Total Millets*
1985-86	22.64	7.32	3.05	1.95	0.16	0.26	5.82
1986-87	19.55	7.30	2.98	1.76	0.29	0.28	6.89
1987-88	19.55	6.88	2.93	1.68	0.21	0.31	6.35
1988-89	18.81	5.62	2.70	1.63	0.30	0.21	6.25
1989-90	19.63	5.87	2.61	1.72	0.35	0.24	8.21
1990-91	18.56	5.41	2.74	1.70	0.27	0.18	8.47
1991-92	21.18	5.12	2.46	1.58	0.34	0.11	7.76
1992-93	21.84	4.84	2.19	1.50	0.43	0.12	7.39
1993-94	23.06	5.06	2.12	1.58	0.38	0.11	6.90
1994-95	22.29	4.32	2.20	1.69	0.65	0.11	6.91

Source: Agro Statistics Directorate of Agriculture, Chennai—1996.

In terms of average area of crops cultivated, Rice, Cholam and Cumbu are the first three ranking crops in the state of Tamil Nadu. In spite of the relatively higher area in the position of food grains, during 1985-86 to 1994-95, it is estimated that the area cultivated by Rice crops had declined from 22.64 lakh hectares in 1985-86 to 22.29 lakh hectares in 1994-95. Similarly for the Cholam crops, the area cultivated had declined from 7.32 lakh hectares to 4.32 lakh hectares and from 3.05 lakh hectares to 2.20 lakh hectares for the cumbu crops during the study period. Thus, the area of major crops are decreased due to the land degradation in Tamil Nadu during the period 1985-86 to 1994-94.

Yield of Major Crops

The production level of major crops in given in Table 2.30.

Table 2.30: Yield of Major Crops is Tamil Nadu from (in Kgs/Ha)

Year	*Rice*	*Cholam*	*Cumbu*	*Ragi*	*Maize*	*Other Millets*	*Total Pulses*
1985-86	2372	1057	1215	1542	1858	615	473
1986-87	2728	902	942	1787	1384	536	453
1987-88	2872	1017	1075	1710	1573	581	451
1988-89	3032	991	1125	1754	1414	619	397
1989-90	3089	1184	1212	1995	1544	542	407
1990-91	3116	1014	1081	1863	1596	556	424
1991-92	3115	1080	1104	1961	1605	545	453
1992-93	3116	1004	1144	1933	1625	568	463
1993-94	2927	960	1121	2095	1618	568	401
1994-95	2392	1134	1708	1953	1522	564	492

Source: Agro Statistics, Directorate of Agriculture, Chennai. 1996.

The yield of rice crops has increased from 2372 kgs per hectare in 1985-86 to 2392 kgs. Per hectare in 1994-95. But the yield of maize had decreased from 1858 kgs per hectare to 1522 kgs per hectare and the millets also declined from 615 kgs per hectare to 564 kgs per hectare during the period from 1985-86 to 1995-96.

Production

The area cultivated and yield of major crops are significantly correlated in Tamil Nadu state during the study period. The production level is given in Table 2.31.

The production of cholam (7.75 lakh M.T. to 4.9 lakh M.T), cumbu (3.71 lakh M.T. to 3.45 lakh M.T.) and of other millets (0.16 lakhs M.T. to 0.03 lakh M.T.) had shown the declining trend during the study period from 1985-86 to 1994-95. But in the case of production of ragi (3 lakh M.T. to 3.42

Table 2.31: Production of Major Crops in Tamil Nadu (in lakhs million tonnes)

Year	*Rice*	*Cholam*	*Cumbu*	*Ragi*	*Magize*	*Other Millets*	*Total Millets*
1985-86	53.70	7.75	3.71	3.00	0.29	0.16	2.75
1986-87	53.33	6.58	2.81	3.15	0.41	0.15	3.12
1887-88	56.14	7.00	3.14	2.68	0.32	0.18	2.83
1988-89	57.04	5.57	3.04	2.86	0.43	0.13	2.48
1989-90	60.63	5.49	2.96	3.16	0.44	0.10	3.34
1990-91	57.82	4.86	2.51	3.11	0.54	0.06	3.59
1991-92	65.96	4.86	2.38	2.91	0.70	0.07	3.51
1992-93	68.06	4.88	3.75	3.31	0.60	0.06	3.43
1993-94	67.49	4.97	3.30	3.38	0.99	0.05	3.4
1994-95	75.59	4.90	3.45	3.42	1.06	0.03	3.39

Source: Agro statistics, Directorate of Agriculture-1996.

lakh M.T., Maize (0.29 lakh M.T. to 1.06 lakh M.T.) and total millets (2.75 lakh M.T.) had shown the increasing trend.

Table 2.32: Consumption of Fertilizers from Cropped Area (N.P.K. & Total) in Tamil Nadu State

	Consumption (in kgs per cropped area in per hectare)			
Year	*N*	*P*	*K*	*Total*
1990-91	64.75 (58.3)	26.11 (20.3)	37.96 (29.4)	128.81 (100.0)
1991-92	70.36	29.02	42.53	141.90
1992-93	64.43	22.86	25.84	113.13
1993-94	57.80	22.50	28.70	109.00
1994-95	64.88 (52.0)	25.59 (20.5)	34.01 (27.5)	124.48 (100.0)

Source: Agro statistics, Directorate of Agriculture, Chennai. 1996.

Note: Figures within parenthesis denotes percentages.

Consumption of Fertilizers

The consumption of fertilizers is another important factor which influence the environment degradation and economic status of the farmers. The fertilizer consumption in the cropped area of Tamil Nadu state is analysed in Table 2.32.

From the table, it is clean that in 1990-91 consumption of fertilizer is 128.81 kgs for cropped Area in Tamil Nadu. It was decreased to 124.48 kgs for cropped area Tamil Nadu secured the first rank and Andhra Pradesh got the second rank from applying the fertilizer in the land.

3

ENVIRONMENTAL DEGRADATION IN STUDY DISTRICTS

The present chapter analyses the district level secondary data regarding geographical area, net area sown, fallow land, net area irrigates, cropping intensity, soil structure cultivable land, uncultivable land for the period of 1993-94 and 2000-01 in order to understand the changes in the environmental situation in the study districts Virdhunagar, Tuticorin and Tirunelveli Districts.

VIRUDHUNAGAR DISTRICT

The climate in Virudhunagar district is hot and dry. The natural annual average rainfall as per the report is 835.0 m.m. The District got a major portion of the rainfall during the north east monsoon. As there are no perennial water resources, agriculture is mainly depending upon seasonal rains. The major crops grown in this district area paddy cholem, cumbu, sugarcane, groundnut, chillies and cotton.

Land Utilisation

The type of soil in Virudhunagar District is explained in Table 3.1.

The soil of Sattur, Srivilliputtur and Aruppukottai is black loams, which is need suited for the cultivation of cotton, chilies and millets. The red soil of Kunnur, Watrap and Natampatti area of Srivilliputtar taluk and Tiruchy Taluk is highly suited for groundnut, gingerly and onion. The size of

Table 3.1: Type of soil in Virudhunagar District (1999-2000)

S. No.	*Type*	*Place in District*
1.	Red loam	Rajaplayam Watrap, Srivilliputtur
2.	Black loam	Tiruchuly, Kariapatti Sathur, Sriviliputtur, Aruppukottai, Virudhunagar
3.	Sandy coastal Alluviam Red Sandy Soil	Narikudi, Kariapatti

Source: Soil Testing lab, Agricultural Department, Virudhunagar, 2000.

uncultivable land, cultivable waste land and fallow lands in Virudhunagar district during the study period is given in Table 3.2.

Table 3.2: Land Utilisation Pattern in Virudhunagar District (Area in Hectare)

Year	*Uncultivable land*	*Cultivable Waste land*	*Fallow Land*
1985-86	4310 (1.96)	5321 (2.42)	29515 (13.45)
1986-87	4320 (1.96)	5791 (2.64)	31417 (14.32)
1987-88	4326 (1.97)	5804 (2.64)	30992 (14.12)
1988-89	4325 (1.97)	5813 (2.65)	29988 (13.67)
1989-90	4324 (1.97)	6518 (2.97)	31816 (14.50)
1990-91	4324 (1.97)	6715 (3.96)	47620 (21.70)
1991-92	4324 (1.97)	6893 (3.14)	42543 (19.39)

(Contd...)

Year	Uncultivable and	Cultivable Waste land	Fallow Land
1992-93	4324 (1.97)	6871 (3.13)	49647 (22.63)
1993-94	4320 (1.96)	6873 (3.13)	43913 (20.01)
1994-95	4319 (1.96)	6878 (3.13)	48771 (22.23)

Source: Department of Agriculture and Engineering, District Collectorate, Virudhunagar. 2000.

Note: Figures within parenthesis denotes the percentage to the total area.

Table 3.2 shows that the size of uncultivable land has increased from 4310 hectare (1.96 per cent) in 1985-86 to 4317 hectare (1.96 per cent) in 1994-95. The uncultivable land area has increased due to the pollution of land and scarcity of water.

The area of cultivable wasteland had increased from 5321 hectare (2.42 per cent) to 6878 hectare (3.13 per cent) during the study period from 1985-86 to 1994-95. The cultivable wasteland has increased year by year due to degradation and land pollution.

The fallow land had increased from 29515 hectare (13.45 per cent) in 1985-86 to 48771 hectare (22.23) in 1994.95. Nearly 10000 hectare of land had not used due to the wastages covered in the land. It is highly controlled the yield of crop during the study period.

Cropping Pattern

The net area sown of the Virudhunagar district is explained in Table 3.3. Table 3.3 explains that net area sown has increased from 93568 hectare (42.65 per cent) in 1985-86 to 107808 hectare in 1994-95. The net area sown had increased due to the efforts of the Government in developing irrigation facilities through major and minor irrigation projects.

Table 3.3: Net Area Sown in Virudhunagar District

Year	*Area*	*Percent*	*Year*	*Area*	*Percent*
1985-86	93568	42.65	1990-91	99857	45.52
1986-87	93216	42.49	1991-92	106968	48.76
1987-88	94111	42.90	1992-93	100514	45.82
1988-89	96767	44.11	1993-94	109312	49.83
1989-90	99910	45.54	1994-95	107808	49.14

Source: Department of Agricultural and Engineering, District Collectorate, Virudhunagar. 2000.

Note: Per cent refers to the percentage of net area sown to the total area.

The cropped area wise in Virudhunagar district is found in Table 3.4.

Table 3.4: Cropped Area in Virudhunagar District (In hectare)

Year	*Cropped Area*	*Geographical Area*
1985-86	269381 (59.61)	451893
1986-87	248597 (56.18)	442485
1987-88	233687 (52.81)	442485
1988-89	218111 (49.29)	442485
1989-90	273126 (61.73)	442485
1990-91	209964 (48.69)	431211
1991-92	187415 (43.46)	431211
1992-93	183953 (42.66)	431211
1993-94	184085 (42.69)	431211
1994-95	191973 (44.52)	431211

Sources: 'G' Return 1999-2000.

Note: Figures within parenthesis denotes percentage.

Table 3.4 shows that there is a declining trend in cropped area in Virudhunagar district. During the study period, of the total geographical area, the cropped area had declined from 269381 hectares (59.61 per cent) in 1985-86 to 191973 hectares (44.52 hectares) in 1994-95.

Of the commercial crops of the district, the most important crop is cotton which is used to be stable crop in the black soils of Sattur, Srivilliputtur and Aruppukottai taluks. However, the trend of cotton cultivation has been declined in recent years. Gingerly and groundnut are the two prominent oil seeds extensively raised in Aruppukottai block.

The crop wise area cultivated in Virudhunagar district is explained in table 3.5.

Table 3.5: Crop wise Area Cultivated in Virudhunagar District (in hectare)

Year	*Paddy*	*Cotton*	*Ragi*	*Gingerly*	*Groundnut*	*Sugar*
1985-86	15929	11993	1216	3878	7936	2211
1986-87	16121	10110	1173	3912	8132	2817
1887-88	18161	40693	1105	3847	8864	2901
1988-89	21155	9726	1201	3965	8915	2920
1989-90	20155	7811	1147	4810	9000	3142
1990-91	22103	7913	1123	4164	9410	2927
1991-92	26592	8010	1055	4248	8412	3010
1992-93	28563	8098	4248	8412	9546	3310
1993-94	27015	8145	1011	4110	10111	3419
1994-95	28905	8214	1035	4332	9877	3307

Source: Department of Agricultural and Engineering, District Collectorate, Virudhunagar, 2000.

The cultivable area had increased in Virudhunagar district over the past 10 years, due to the development of crop varieties that were supplied through Agricultural Department. The different type of cropping system had practiced in traditional agriculture. The system involving only a few crops which are highly nutrients depleting but high yielding. The area of paddy crop has decreased from 159293 hectare in

1985-86 to 28905 hectare in 1994-95 but the area of gingerly has increased from 3878 hectare in 1985-86 to 4332 in 1994-95. The cholum, ragi, groundnut, sugar which were regular components of cropping system which have largely been phased out in highly protective areas due to poor economic returns and replaced by high yielding paddy, groundnut, cholum, etc., in Virudhuinagar District.

Irrigation Efficiency

The year wise area irrigation in Virudhunagar district is explained in Table 3.6.

Table 3.6: Irrigation Efficiency in Virudhunagar District (In hectare)

Year	*Net area Irrigated*	*Gross area Irrigated*	*% of more than Net area irrigates*
1985-86	31110 (82.10)	37754	17.59
1986-87	32645 (95.69)	34116	4.31
1987-88	33515 (99.03)	33842	0.96
1988-89	31116 (90.94)	34217	9.06
1989-90	32810 (93.36)	35145	6.64
1990-91	32515 (91.02)	35721	8.97
1991-92	32167 (88.18)	36478	11.81
1992-93	33910 (94.69)	35810	5.30
1993-94	33910 (88.98)	38110	11.02
1994-95	34012 (96.86)	35113	3.13

Source: Department of Agricultural Engineering District Collectorate, Virudhunagar, 2000.

Note: Figures within parenthesis denotes percentages to the Gross area Irrigated.

Out of the total irrigated area, only 40% irrigated by tanks. The remaining areas are receiving well irrigation. Table 3.6 shows that the net area irrigated had increased from 31110 hectare in 1985-86 to 34012 hectare in 1994-95 in Vidhunagar district. But the gross area irrigated had decreased from 37754 hectares in 1985-86 to 35113 hectare in 1994-95.

Production

The crop wise production level in Virudhunagar district is shown in Table 3.7.

Table 3.7: Crop wise Production Level in Virudhunagar District (000' tonnes)

Year	*Paddy*	*Cholam*	*Ragi*	*Gingerly*	*Groundnut*	*Sugarcane*
1985-86	71.6	16.8	4.2	1.0	11.3	286.7
1986-87	66.6	15.2	3.9	0.7	12.10	219.0
1988-89	68.1	14.5	3.9	0.8	12.3	290.2
1989-90	72.3	14.7	4.6	0.9	13.0	303.9
1990-91	71.2	11.0	3.4	1.1	13.3	292.4
1991-92	74.5	16.9	2.2	1.2	12.4	300.1
1992-93	79.4	14.9	2.4	1.0	13.1	336.0
1993-94	81.7	15.1	2.5	1.4	4.1	238.9
1994-95	80.5	13.2	2.2	1.4	13.5	337.0

Source: 'G' return 1999-2000.

The production level had increased in all crops except the Cholam crop in Vidhunagar district during the study period. Despite, there is a declining trend in cropped area, due to the growth of net area irrigated, the level of production had increased in all crops in this district.

Table 3.8: Consumption of Chemical Fertiliser and Pesticides in 1999-2000

Fertiliser	*(in M.T.)*	*Pesticides*	
Nitrogen (N)	7319 (55.77)	Dust (k.g.)	10544 (23.62)
Phosphatic (p 205)	2940 (22.40)	liquid (G.T.)	21901 (49.06)
Pottassic (k20)	2864 (21.83)	Area 000 tonnes	12198 (27.32)
Total	13123 (100.00)		44643 (100.00)

Source: Joint Director of Agricultural, Virudhunagar. 2000.

Note: Figures within parenthesis denotes percentages.

Use of Chemicals

The use of chemical fertilizer in agriculture in Virudhunagar district is depicted in Table 3.8.

It is clear that the use of nitrogen (55.77 per cent) fertiliser and liquid (49.06 per cent) pesticides dominated in the agricultural production in Virdhunagar district of Tamil Nadu.

TIRUNELVELI DISTRICT

Land Utilisation Pattern

The district has one fourth (23.34 per cent) of its total geographical area (6,42,728 hectare) under wet cultivation of net area sown and, 32.83 per cent of the area is cultivated

Table 3.9: Land Utilisation Pattern in Tirunelveli District (in Hectare)

Year	*Uncultivable waste land*	*Cultivable waste land*	*Current fallow land*
1985-86	20716 (3.22)	70628 (10.99)	15152 (2.35)
1986-87	20716 (3.22)	20310 (10.94)	16815 (2.61)
1987-88	20716 (3.22)	71363 (11.11)	17610 (2.74)
1988-89	20716 (3.22)	71963 (11.20)	13343 (2.07)
1989-90	20863 (3.24)	72640 (11.30)	14421 (2.24)
1990-91	21791 (3.39)	71110 (11.07)	16526 (2.57)
1991-92	21791 (3.39)	72336 (11.26)	39740 (6.18)
1992-93	21791 (3.39)	71885 (11.19)	17410 (2.71)
1993-94	21791 (3.39)	72234 (11.24)	24310 (3.78)
1994-95	21791 (3.39)	72197 (11.24)	18582 (2.89)

Source: Department of Agriculture and Engineering, District Collectorate, Tirunelveli 2001.

Note: Figures within parenthesis denotes the percentage to the total area.

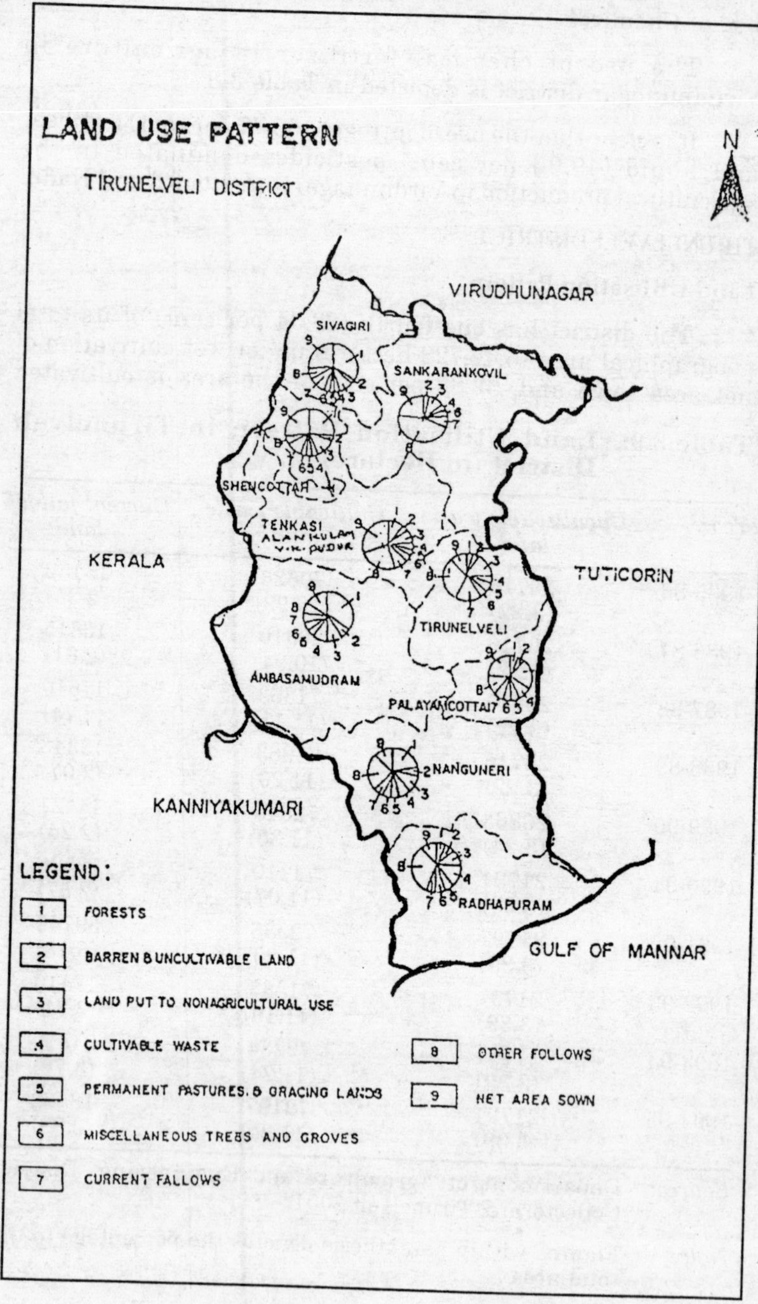
LAND USE PATTERN
TIRUNELVELI DISTRICT
N
VIRUDHUNAGAR
SIVAGIRI
SANKARANKOVIL
SHENCOTTAH
TENKASI
ALANKULAM
V.K. PUDUR
KERALA
TUTICORIN
TIRUNELVELI
AMBASAMUDRAM
PALAYANKOTTAI
NANGUNERI
KANNIYAKUMARI
RADHAPURAM
GULF OF MANNAR
LEGEND:
1 FORESTS
2 BARREN & UNCULTIVABLE LAND
3 LAND PUT TO NONAGRICULTURAL USE
4 CULTIVABLE WASTE
5 PERMANENT PASTURES & GRACING LANDS
6 MISCELLANEOUS TREES AND GROVES
7 CURRENT FALLOWS
8 OTHER FOLLOWS
9 NET AREA SOWN

more than once. The low percentage of cultivation in the district could be attributed to the facts that as much as 18.24 per cent of the area is covered with forests and 3.73 per cent of land are barren and uncultivable.

Of the forest area 1,24,321 Ha, Farm forestry plantations covered 9,158 Ha. And Economic plantations extent to 2,150 Ha. Quick growing plantations are raised in 1,361 Ha. During the period from 1985-86 to 1994-95 in Tirunelveli district, the uncultivable waste land had increased from 3.22 per cent (20716 hectares) to 3.39 per cent (21791 hectares) of the total geographical area. The cultivable waste land and current fallow lands are 72197 hectare (11.24 per cent) and 18582 hectares (2.89 per cent) in Tirunelveli district. This figures shows that there is an increasing trend of the cultivable waste land and current fallow lands in Tirunelveli district during the study period.

Soil erosion in general is one of the crucial problems of agriculture but it is more so in agriculturally developed region due to excessive uses of irrigation, mismanagement of the flow of water in the canals. The improper maintenance of canals have led to the massive underground percolation of water. In, Tirunelveli District, wastes fallow lands are more than 70000 Ha. These waste and fallow lands are increasing every year. The net area sown in diminishing year by year. The fast deteriorating ecological balance in this district has to be essentially avoided further.

Cropping Pattern

The net area sown in Tirunelveli district are explained in Table 3.10.

Table 3.10: Net Area Sown in Tirunelveli District (in hectare)

Year	*Area*	*Percent*	*Year*	*Area*	*Percent*
1985-86	15225	2.37	1990-91	15410	2.39
1986-87	15346	2.38	1991-92	16343	2.54
1987-88	15810	2.46	1992-93	16978	2.64
1988-89	16197	2.52	1993-94	17119	2.66
1989-90	16207	2.52	1994-95	17226	2.68

Source: Assistant Statistical Office, District Collectorate, Tirunelveli. 2000.

Table 3.11: Area under Selected Crops in Tirunelveli District (in hectare)

Year	*Paddy*	*Cholum*	*Ragi*	*Pulses*	*Cotton*	*Groundnut*	*Sugar*
1985-86	63241	2411	813	23198	1949	8080	3763
1986-87	63243	2413	895	24567	1777	8513	3840
1987-88	65616	2655	980	29115	1949	8727	4516
1988-89	73617	2764	919	30812	1768	8813	3812
1989-90	88246	2941	998	28515	1843	9048	3952
1990-91	75642	3018	1008	29444	1916	9186	4428
1991-92	64312	2943	1100	31868	2155	9217	4155
1992-93	84913	2815	1217	30125	2048	9617	4410
1993-94	80992	3010	1319	31617	2273	9585	4390
1994-95	76310	3017	1486	32801	2285	9421	4387

Source: Department of Agriculture and Engineering, District Collectorate, Tirunelveli 2001.

The area used for cultivation for different selected crops during the study period is exhibited in Table 3.11. The study found that cultivable area for all crops have increased during the study periods. The growth of wet land crops like paddy and sugar have a slow growth rate. But the dry lands crops like cholam, ragi, have increased at a higher rate. The

Table 3.12: Cropping Intensity in Tirunelveli District (in hectare)

Year	*Area*	*Percentage**	*Year*	*Area*	*Percentage**
1985-86	139.65	0.02	1990-91	128.12	0.01
1986-87	138.13	0.02	1991-92	129.55	0.02
1987-88	137.67	0.02	1992-93	129.37	0.02
1988-89	136.58	0.02	1993-94	128.16	0.01
1989-90	130.58	0.02	1994-95	127.05	0.01

Source: Department of Agriculture and Engineering, District Collectorate, Tirunelveli. 2001

Note: *In total Geographical area.

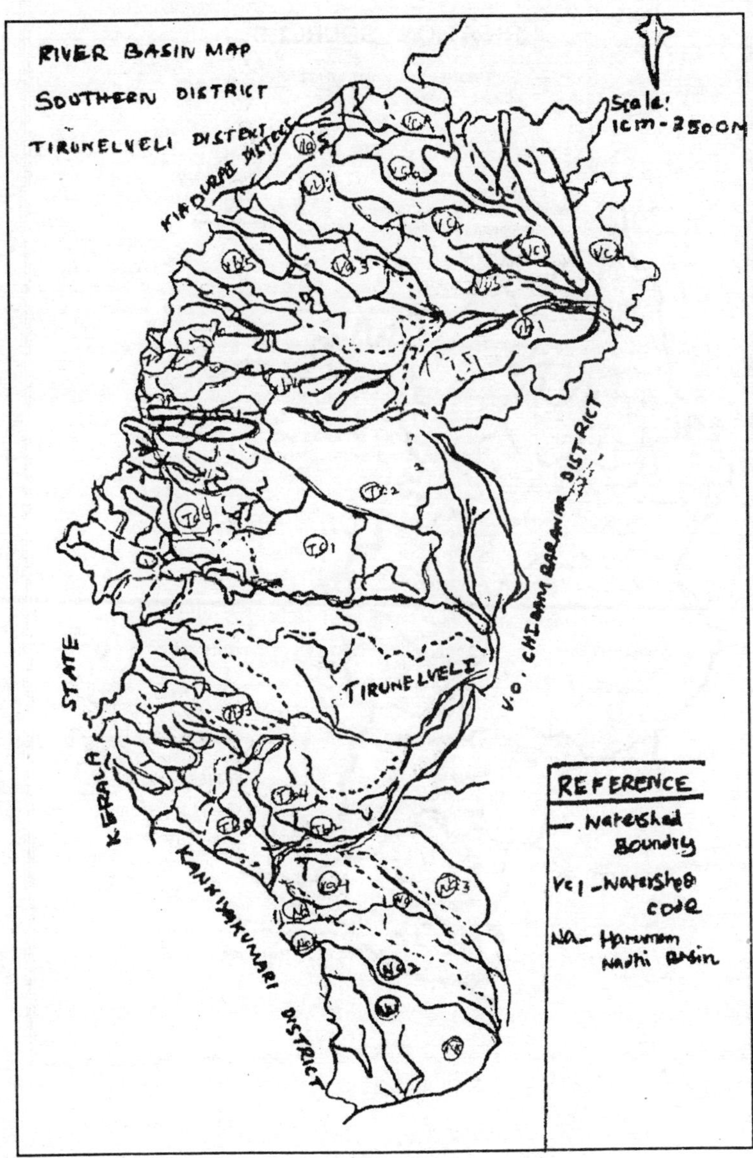
RIVER BASIN MAP
SOUTHERN DISTRICT
TIRUNELVELI DISTRICT
Scale: 1cm-2500M
KERALA STATE
TIRUNELVELI
V.O. CHIDAMBARANAR DISTRICT
KANNIYAKUMARI DISTRICT
REFERENCE
Watershed Boundry
Vc1 _Watershed code
NA- Hanuman Nadhi Basin

IRRIGATION SOURCES
TIRUNELVELI DISTRICT
N
Virudhunagar district
6980
Sivagiri
133
Sankarankovil
22720
255
22549
166
15-00
902
185-60
Shencottai
344
Tenkasi
Tuticorin district
6048
198
Kerala State
5001
403
Tirunelveli
146
1400
37-00
25-00
Ambasamudram
Palayan-cottai
99-40
6670
318
Nanguneri
66-00
11050
2-00
Kanyakumari district
Radhapuram
285
GULF OF MANNAR
REFERENCE
WELL (Nos)
TANK (Nos)
CANAL (kms)
PROJECT AREA

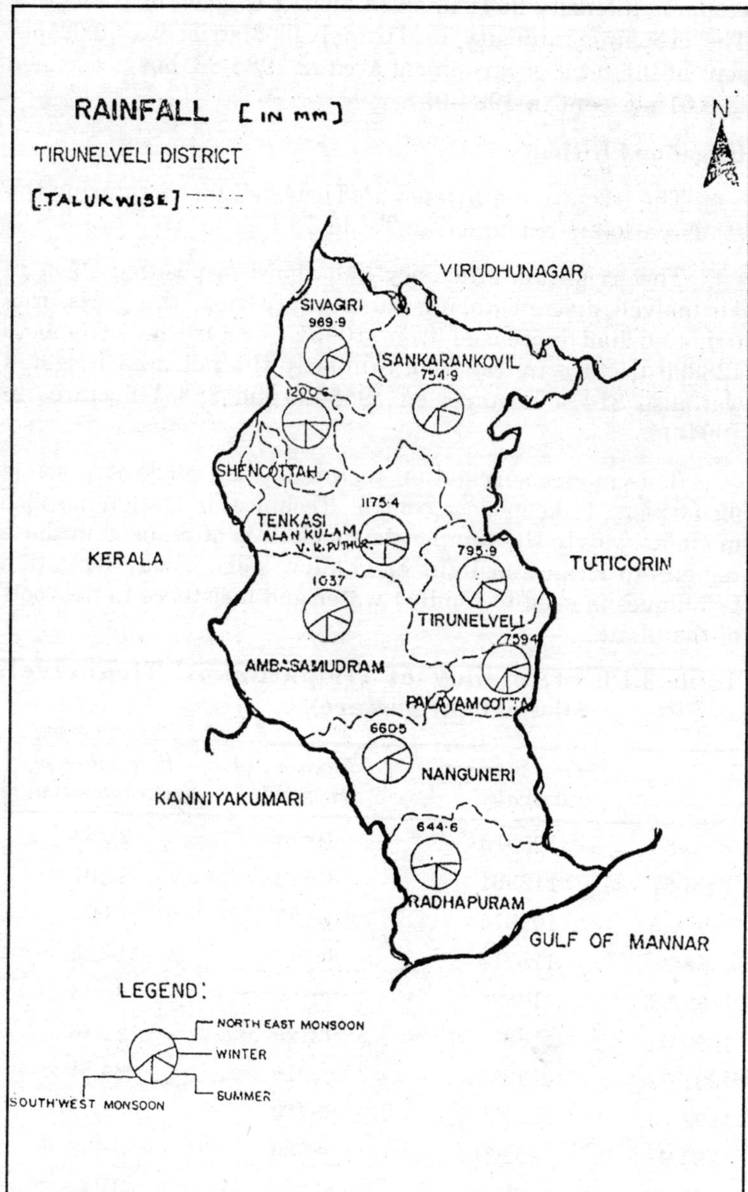
RAINFALL [IN mm]
TIRUNELVELI DISTRICT
[TALUKWISE]
N
VIRUDHUNAGAR
SIVAGIRI
969·9
SANKARANKOVIL
754·9
1200·6
SHENCOTTAH
1175·4
TENKASI
ALAN KULAM
V. K. PUTHUR
KERALA
795·9
TUTICORIN
1037
TIRUNELVELI
759·4
AMBASAMUDRAM
PALAYAMCOTTA
660·5
NANGUNERI
KANNIYAKUMARI
644·6
RADHAPURAM
GULF OF MANNAR
LEGEND:
NORTH EAST MONSOON
WINTER
SUMMER
SOUTH WEST MONSOON

cropping intensity in Tirunelveli district is given in Table 3.12. The cropping intensity in Tirunelveli district was 0.02 per cent of the total geographical area in 1985-86, but it declined to 0.01 per cent in 1994-95.

Irrigation Efficiency

The irrigation efficiency in Tirnelveli district during the study period is explained in Table 3.13.

The irrigation efficiency had shown a positive effect in Tirunelveli district during the study period, the gross area irrigated had increased from 105513 hectare in 1985-86 to 128809 hectare in 1994-95. Similarly the net area irrigated was also 81414 hectares in 1985-86 and 88331 hectares in 1994-95.

This modern irrigation technique has made it possible for farmers, to keep close control. Technical irrigation has also made its way to the temperate zones. It is often used in these regions to irrigation light or shallow soils. Today irrigation techniques is used to conduct water and insistence to the roots of the plant.

Table 3.13: Efficiency of Irrigation in Tirunelveli District (in hectare)

Year	*Gross Area Irrigated*	*Net area Irrigated*	*Percentage in more than net area*
1985-86	105513	81414	22.83
1986-87	112961	80112	29.07
1987-88	109615	84325	23.07
1988-89	118715	86515	27.12
1989-90	118826	90150	24.13
1990-91	118814	92125	22.46
1991-92	118814	89919	24.31
1992-93	128809	88410	31.36
1993-94	128809	88330	31.42
1994-95	128809	88331	31.42

Source: Department of Agriculture and Engineering District Collectorate, Tirunelveli. 2001.

Agricultural Yield

The agricultural yield and productivity per hectare in Tirunelveli district during the study period is anslysed in Tables 3.14 and 3.15. The level of production of the selected crops in the study district had declined during the study period. But the productivity per hectare has increased for all crops except pulses.

Table 3.14: Production of Selected Crops in Tirunelveli District: (in Million tonnes)

Year	*Paddy*	*Cholum*	*Ragi*	*Pulses*	*Cotton*	*Groundnut*	*Sugar*
1985-86	269084	6351	3388	12997	4780	10127	49335
1986-87	63243	2413	895	24567	3345	8513	3840
1987-88	65616	2655	980	29115	1949	8727	4516
1988-89	73617	2764	919	30812	1768	8813	3812
1989-90	88246	2941	998	28515	1843	9048	3952
1990-91	75642	3018	1008	29444	1916	9186	4428
1991-92	64312	2943	1100	31868	2155	9217	4155
1992-93	84913	2815	1217	30125	2048	9617	4410
1993-94	77621	3010	1319	31617	2273	9585	4390
1994-95	76310	3017	1486	32801	2285	9421	4387

Source: Department of Agriculture and Engineering District Collectorate, Tirunelveli. 2001.

Table 3.15: Productivity of Selected Crops in Tirunelveli District (per Tonne kg/hectare)

Year	*Paddy*	*Cholum*	*Ragi*	*Pulses*	*Cotton*	*Groundnut*	*Sugar*
1985-86	2.937	1.581	1.985	0.515	1.74	0.730	8.98
1986-87	3.945	2.008	1.999	0.619	1.74	0.674	9.12
1987-88	2.694	2.196	2.003	0.554	1.87	0.951	13.4
1988-89	3.001	2.009	2.007	0.601	1.84	0.753	9.99
1989-90	3.513	2.551	2.210	0.600	2.04	0.965	10.1
1990-91	3.865	2.995	2.943	0.657	1.99	1.000	13.8
1991-92	3.391	2.119	2.531	0.712	2.01	1.001	11.5
1992-93	4.324	2.004	2.153	0.875	2.03	2.046	13.1
1993-94	4.345	2.313	2.915	0.916	2.21	1.913	12.6
1994-95	4.347	2.424	2.400	0.407	2.25	1.286	12.5

Source: Department of Agriculture and Engineering, District Collectorate, Tirunelveli. 2001.

TUTICORIN DISTRICT

The climate is hot and dry. Tuticorin District has a coastal line of 135 kms. And territorial waters covering thousands of hectares. The district particularly in and around Tuticorin has the major salt production in the state and contributes 30% of the total salt production of the country. The mixed landscape of the sea and the wastelands has imbibed some special traits in the character of the sons of the soil.

The net area sown in Tuticorin district was 203096 hectares in 1985-86 and it increased to 208053 hectares in 1994-95. Similarly the uncultivable waste land area had also increased from 68910 hectare in 1985-86 to 70159 hectare in 1994-95.

The uncultivable wasteland had increased from 68,910 hectare to 70159 hectare during period 1985-86 to 1994-95 i.e. 1249 hectare was increased during period. Moreover, uncultivable waste land also increased during the period due to the land degradation.

The uncultivable land had increased from 19855 hectare in 1985-86 to 19954 hectare in 1994-95 due to the erosion of the land. It is very meager level to the total geographical land of Tuticorin district. The proportion of barren and uncultivable land is extremely high in the Tuticorin district because of hard rocky surface, occurrence of land slides, soil and wind erosion.

Table 3.16 explains that current fallow land had decreased from 45214 hectare to 40884 hectare land during period from 1985-86 to 1994-95 due to soil erosion, land slides and drought prone conditions. This, however, indicate that there is a good scope for extending the proper utilisation of fallow lands and reclamation of cultivable waste land, provided, adequate irrigation facilities are to be made available and land development programmes may be taken up vigorously.

Table 3.16: Land Utilisation Pattern in Tuticorin District (in hectare)

Year	*Net area sown*	*Uncultivable waste land*	*Uncultivable land*	*Current fallow land*
1985-86	203096 (45.03)	68910 (15.28)	19855 (4.40)	45214 (10.02)
1986-87	218885 (48.53)	68927 (15.28)	19896 (4.41)	45214 (10.02)
1987-88	218585 (48.47)	69513 (15.41)	19900 (4.41)	46208 (10.24)
1988-89	208128 (46.15)	69513 (15.41)	19909 (4.41)	46319 (10.27)
1989-90	218855 (48.53)	69705 (15.45)	19915 (4.41)	46208 (10.24)
1990-91	208010 (46.12)	69894 (15.49)	19936 (4.42)	45250 (10.03)
1991-92	208054 (46.13)	69894 (15.49)	19944 (4.42)	48142 (10.67)
1992-93	206889 (45.27)	69894 (15.49)	19944 (4.42)	48142 (10.67)
1993-94	219104 (48.58)	70159 (15.55)	19944 (4.42)	40384 (8.95)
1994-95	208053 (46.13)	70159 (15.55)	19955 (4.42)	40884 (9.06)

Source: Department of Agriculture and Engineering District Collectorate, Tuticorin. 2001.

Cropping Pattern and Irrigation

The main food crop is paddy, in Tuticorin district. Of the total area of 450954 hectare, 185048 hectare are brought under the cultivation of different crops which is nearly 42% of the total area. The important food crops are paddy, cholum, cumbu, ragi, varagu, and commercial crops like cotton, chilies, sugarcane and groundnut. The different sources of Irrigation are channel tanks, which covers 45199 hectares and the rest of out of this 21941 hectares were covered by wells.

The area under multiple cropping may increase in future but to a limited extent because of more area being under perennial crops. The cropped area is increased from 219381 hectare in 1985-86 to 222471 hectare in 1994-95 in Tuticorin district thereby raising the cropped area to 3090 hectares. The total cropped area for the study period is given in Table 3.17 and the area under various crops in Tuticorin district is exhibited in Table 3.18.

Table 3.17: Cropped Area in Tuticorin District (in Hectare)

Year	*Cropped Area*	*Percentage in Geographical area*
1985-86	219381	48.64
1986-87	219684	48.71
1987-88	219684	48.71
1988-89	209736	46.50
1989-90	219222	48.61
1990-91	209856	46.53
1991-92	217418	48.21
1992-93	219213	48.61
1993-94	222471	49.33
1994-95	222471	49.33

Source: Department of Agriculture and Engineering, District Collectorate, Tuticorin. 2001.

The area under crops cultivation is a fair index to assess the district agricultural development position. During 1985-86, area of paddy crop cultivation in the District worked out to 31763 hectare as against 30120 hectare in 1994-95. The area of gingelly crops cultivation worked out to 7233 hectare as against 6994 hectare during the study period. The area of ground nut cultivation is worked out to 2889 hectare in 1985-86 as against 2723 hectare in 1994-985. The area of cotton cultivation worked out to 31486 hectare as against 30670 hectare. The area of sugar cultivation worked out to 212 hectare as against 195 hectare and area of chilies cultivation worked out to 16082 hectare as against 16416 hectare in 1994-

Table 3.18: Area under Crops in Tuticorin District (in hectare)

Year	*Paddy*	*Gingerly*	*Groundnut*	*Cotton*	*Sugar*	*Chilies*
1985-86	31763	7235	2889	31486	212	16082
1986-87	30675	7155	2880	32481	201	16080
1987-88	29611	7058	2780	31313	202	17110
1988-89	30107	7168	2843	29425	198	15853
1989-90	31919	7010	2985	30464	196	14533
1990-91	30008	6513	3000	26153	194	15156
1991-92	30100	6989	3004	28344	191	15927
1992-93	30108	6990	2953	28217	195	15156
1993-94	31801	6998	2824	31412	195	15271
1994-95	30120	6994	2723	30670	195	16416

Source: Department of Agriculture and Engineering District Collectorate, Tuticorin. 2001.

95. The area of crop cultivation is highly varied from one crop to other crop. The area under crops cultivated had fallen for all crops except chilies in Titicorin District. The net area sown is explained in Table 3.19.

Table 3.19: Net Area Sown in Tuticorin District

Year	*Net area sown*	*Gross area*	*Percentage as more than in Net area wowen*
1985-86	48793	60412	19.23
1986-87	48793	59810	18.41
1987-88	48805	59613	18.13
1988-89	48795	59623	18.16
1989-90	48823	59313	17.68
1990-91	48818	59810	18.37
1991-92	48820	59724	18.25
1992-93	48823	59724	18.25
1993-94	48823	59725	18.25
1994-95	48823	59724	18.25

Source: Department of Agriculture and Engineering, District Collectorate, Tuticorin. 2001.

In spite of improvement in irrigation facilities, a substantial portion of the cropped area had declined in Tuticorin due to the rainfall failure or late commencement of rainy seasons which are quite common occurrence and affect the agriculture adversely. Increasing irrigation facilities is necessary for a good harvest under intensive cultivation and for raising more area under cultivation. In 1985-86, about 60412 hectare and it was decreased to 59724 hectare of area benefited by irrigation. The net area sown accounted for 48793 hectare in 1985-86 and 48823 hectare in 1994-95 in the district. More than 50 per cent of the net area sown was under irrigation which appears to be due to concentration of surface irrigation efficiency in the district.

Agricultural Yield

The level of agricultural production in Tuticorin district during the study period is given in Table 3.20.

Table 3.20: Production Under Crops in Tuticorin District (M. Tonnes)

Year	*Paddy*	*Cholam*	*Ragi*	*Cotton*	*Gingelly*	*Chilies*
1985-86	55.82	15.02	0.93	11.97	3.25	10.68
1986-87	54.28	14.98	0.83	12.97	3.13	10.64
1987-88	53.04	14.03	0.91	11.85	3.12	11.64
1988-89	54.26	13.14	0.81	9.72	2.87	9.86
1989-90	55.82	10.16	0.66	11.11	2.85	9.99
1990-91	53.23	12.01	0.73	10.99	2.81	8.97
1991-92	54.10	12.03	0.72	9.83	2.87	9.79
1992-93	54.00	12.12	0.66	10.95	2.74	9.87
1993-94	56.51	12.43	0.73	12.63	2.74	10.48
1994-95	54.17	12.43	0.81	11.13	2.74	10.51

Source: Department of Agriculture and Engineering, District Collectorate, Tuticorin. 2001.

In 1985-86, total production consists of 55.82 M. Tonnes of paddy, 15.02 M. Tonnes of Cholam, 0.93 M. Tonnes of Ragi, 11.97 tonnes of cotton, and 3.25 M. Tonnes of gingelly and

10.68 M. Tonnes of chilies. The production of foodgrains had decreased manifold in the last 10 years (1985-86 to 1994-95), because there is no introduction of hybrid rice and other cereals and no use of improved agricultural technology. The productivity level of various crops during the study period in Tuticorin district is explained in Table 3.21.

Table 3.21: Productivity Under Crops in Tuticorin District (kg/per hectare)

Year	*Paddy*	*Cholasm*	*Rsagi*	*Cotton*	*Groundnut*	*Gingelly*	*Chilies*
1985-86	3195	1793	1383	127	1502	198	392
1986-87	3108	1699	1370	131	1947	199	391
1987-88	2995	1683	1360	116	1530	202	413
1988-89	3107	1704	1357	998	1532	200	344
1989-90	3213	1689	1394	100	1533	204	355
1990-91	2998	1413	1385	99	1533	204	307
1991-92	3106	1502	1361	92	1521	205	341

Source: Department of Agriculture and Engineering, District Collectorate, Tuticorin. 2001.

The average yield of paddy, cholam, ragi, cotton, gingelly and chillies yield worked out as 3195, 1793, 1383, 127, 1502, 198, and 392 Kg per hectare 195-0as against the corresponding figure 3108, 1510, 1345, 101, 1516, 207 and 385 kg per hectare in 1994-95 in Tuticorin district. The lower yield of crops in the district is attributed to the worst physical and climatic condition prevalent in the area. A study of the trend of productivity indicates that there is no marked improvement in the average yield of crops during the last 10 years. For instance, the yield of paddy was the order of 3195 kg per hectare in 1985-86 which come down up to 3108 kg per hectare in 1994-95 with the low improvement in irrigation facilities.

Fertilizer Used

After Green Revolution, with the advancement of science and technology, chemical fertilizers play an important role in the agricultural production. The use of chemical fertilizers and pesticides in Tuticorin district is given in Table 3.22.

Table 3.22: Use of Chemical Fertilizers and Pesticides in Tuticorin District (in 1999)

Fertilisers	*000 Tonnes*	*Pesticides*	
Nitrogen	11850	Dusts	6800
Phosphate	44528	Higuid (hit)	8200
Potash	3110	Area (000 Tons)	9895
Total	19485		24895

Source: Department of Agriculture and Engineering District Collectorate, Tuticorin. 2001.

The use of pesticides is necessary for protection of crops and plants against insects, pathogens, seed rodents, etc. Majority of the crops are liable to one or the other type of pest infestation as such the entire cropped area should normally be covered under appropriate plant protection schemes to grow yield. The consumption of chemical fertilizers are 11850 Tonnes Nitrogen (N) 44528 Tonnes phosphate (P205) and 3110 Tonnes potash and a total of 19485 thousand tonnes of chemical fertilizers are used in Tuticorin District.

Impact of Environment Degradation on Rural Poverty

The impact of environment degradation on rural poverty can be studied by comparing the changes in the socio-economic status of the sample respondents and participation level in the field of agriculture by the farmers in the selected study districts. The data collected through the interview schedule are analysed in this chapter. The first part of the chapter dealt with the socio-economic status profile of the respondents and the second part analyse the agricultural changes/ development during the study period in study districts.

CHANGES IN SOCIO-ECONOMIC PROFILE OF THE RESPONDENTS

Socio-economic aspects such as the area, religion, age, marital status, family status, income, expenditure, saving and indebtedness provide a base for studying the impact of any programme. The socio-economic conditions are studied with reference to the respondents and their families. This part attempts to study the socio-economic background of the respondents.

Area

The area wise classification of the respondents is explained in Table 4.1

Table 4.1 reveals that of the total respondents, 150 belong to Virudhunager district, 150 respondents belong to Tuticorin district and 150 respondents belong to Tirunelveli district. It is clear that 254 (46.4 per cent) are small farmers,

122 (27.1 per cent) are marginal farmers and 74 (16.5 per cent) are large farmers. The district wise classification of the respondent shows 97 small farmers, 34 marginal farmers and 19 large farmers in Virudunagar district, 83 small farmers 42 marginal farmers and 25 large farmers in Tuticorin district and 74 small farmers, 46 marginal farmers and 30 large farmers in Tirunelveli district.

Table 4.1: Area-wise Classification of the Sample Respondents

Sl. No.	*Category of farmers*	*Virudunagaer*	*Tuticorin*	*Tirunelveli*	*Total*
1.	Small Farmers	97 (64.7)	83 (55.3)	74 (49.3)	254 (56.4)
2.	Marginal Farmers	34 (22.7)	42 (28.0)	46 (30.7)	122 (27.1)
3.	Large Farmers	19 (12.6)	25 (16.7)	30 (20.0)	74 (16.5)
	Total	150 (100.0)	150 (100.0)	150 (100.0)	450 (100.0)

Source: Computed from Primary data.

Note: Figures within the parenthesis denotes the percentages.

From these figures, it is inferred that the small farmers constitute the higher percentage (56.4 per cent) (254 farmers) and large farmers form the lowest percentage among the groups of farmers.

Age

The age wise classification of the sample respondents is exhibited in Table 4.2.

Table 4.2 shows that at the gross level, 68.8 per cent of the respondents belong to the age group of 26-50 years, 29.7 per cent belongs to the age group of 51 above and years and the remaining 3.5 per cent belongs to the age group of 15-25 years.

At the block level, 108 respondents belong to the age group of 26-50 years, 36 respondents belong to the age group of 51 years and above years and 108 respondents belong to

Table 4.2: Age-wise Classification of the Sample Respondents

Age	*Name of the Block*			
	Aruppukottai	*Tenkasi*	*Srivaikundan*	*Total*
18-25	6 (4.0)	3 (2.0)	7 (3.7)	16 (3.5)
26-50	108 (72.0)	90 (60.0)	112 (74.6)	310 (68.8)
51 & above	36 (24.0)	57 (38.0)	41 (27.3)	124 (29.7)
Total	150 (100.0)	150 (100.0)	150 (100.0)	450(100.0)

Source: Computer from primary data 2001.

Note: Figures within the parenthesis denotes the percentage.

the age group of 15-25 years in Aruppukottai block of Virudunagar district, 90 respondents belong to the age group of 26-50 years, 57 respondents belong to the age group of 51 and above years and 3 respondents belong to the age group of 15-25 years in Tenkasi block of Tirunelveli district. 112 respondents belong to the age group of 26-50 years, 45 respondents belong to the age group of 51 and above and 7 respondents belong to the age group of 15-25 years in Srivaikundam block of Tuticorin district.

Table 4.3: Educational Status of the Sample Respondents

Sl. No.	*Status*	*Name of the Block*			
		Aruppukottai	*Tenkasi*	*Srivaikundan*	*Total*
1.	Illiterate	36 (24.0)	61 (40.0)	51 (34.0)	148 (32.8)
2.	Primary	73 (48.6)	45 (30.0)	64 (42.7)	182 (40.5)
3.	Secondary	26 (17.4)	31 (20.7)	17 (11.3)	74 (16.5)
4.	Dip/hig	15 (10.0)	13 (8.7)	18 (12.0)	46 (10.2)
	Total	150(100.0)	150(100.0)	150(100.0)	450 (100.0)

Source: Computed from primary data.

Note: Figures within the parenthesis denotes the percentage.

Education

Education is one of the most pertinent factor that affects human behaviour and their occupational status. The literacy level of the respondents is depicted in Table 4.3

It is observed that at the gross level, (32.8 per cent) respondents are illiterate, while 182 (40.5 per cent) respondents are having completed secondary education and just 46 (10.2 per cent) have studied upto diploma and higher education. This clearly shows that more than 32.8 per cent of the respondents are not having proper education.

Sex

The sex wise distribution of the sample respondents are presented in Table 4.4. It is seen that of the 450 respondents, 421 are male and 429 are female and this forms 93.5 per cent and 6.5 per cent respectively. In the category of block level, the sample respondent consists of 96 percentage of male and 4 percentage of female in Aruppukottai block of Virudunagar district, 93.3 per cent male farmers and 6.7 per cent female farmers in Tenkasi block of Tirunelveli district and 91.3 per cent of male farmers and 8.7 per cent of female farmers in Srivaikundam block level of Tuticorin district. It could be inferred the highest per cent of farmers are male in the three blocks including small, marginal and large and in the lowest per cent of farmers are female in the each block.

Table 4.4: Sex-Wise Classification of the Sample Respondents

Sl. No.	*Name of the Block*	*Sex*		
		Male	*Female*	*Total*
1.	Arupukottai	144 (96)	6 (4)	150 (100)
2.	Tenkasi	140 (93.3)	10 (6.7)	150 (100)
3.	Srivaikundam	137 (91.3)	13 (8.7)	150 (100)
	Grand Total	421 (93.5)	29 (6.5)	450 (100)

Source: Computed from primary data.

Note: Figures within the parenthesis denotes the percentages.

Family Size

Table 4.5: Average Family Size of the Sample Respondent

Sl. No.	*Name of Blocks*	*Small Farmers*	*Marginal Farmers*	*Large Farmers*	*Average*
1.	Aruppukottai	2.75	3.47	3.52	3.53
2.	Tenkasi	3.35	3.84	3.93	3.70
3.	Srivikundam	3.77	3.16	3.80	3.57
	Average	3.62	3.49	3.75	3.62

Source: Computed from primary data.

The average family size of the sample respondents are given in Table 4.5. It shows that the average family size of small farmers is 3.62, the average family size of marginal farmers is 3.49 and the average family size of large farmers is 3.75. At the category level, the large farmers had possessed large number of average family size (3.75) in these three sample districts, and the large number of family size occupied (3.70) in Tenkasi among the sample blocks.

Assets

Table 4.6: Average Assets Level of the Sample Respondents (1993-94)

Sl. No.	*Assets*	*Small*		*Marginal*		*Large*		*Total*	
		Q.	*Value*	*Q.*	*Value*	*Q*	*Value*	*Q*	*Value*
1. Land									
2.	(i) Wet	2.20	18500	4.33	36410	7.54	62657	4.69	39189
	(ii) Dry	1.81	9300	3.85	19781	6.71	34475	4.12	63557
3.	Building	2.4	28620	2.3	17843	2.8	32827	2.5	21185
4.	Animals	3.85	5840	1.63	3485	3.13	4813	2.3	26430
4.	Agri-Implants	3.1	1120	4.7	4143	5.2	19875	4.3	4713
5.	Vehicles	1.4	3976	2.3	7732	2.9	941	2.2	7039
6.	Furniture	0.7	1050	1.2	2114	2.3	3325	1.4	7039
7.	Jewels	4.4	13875	8.5	26443	11.6	36088	8.1	2163
8.	Others	—	1800	—	4215	—	13427	—	25468
	Total		84081		122166		330594		196783

Source: Computed from Primary data

Note: Value in Rupees Quantity in Nos./acres

The particulars of the assets owned by the respondents (farmers) are given in Table 4.6. It is clear that the average land owned by the small farmers was 2.20 acres of wet land and 1.81 acres of dry land, at the value of Rs. 18500 and Rs. 9300 respectively. The marginal farmers possessed the 4.33 acres of wet land and 3.85 acres of dry land at the value of Rs. 36419 and Rs. 19781 respectively. The average land owned by the large farmers was 7.54 acres of wet land and 7.71 acre of dry land at the value of Rs. 62657 and Rs. 34475 respectively in the year 1993-94.

Table 4.7: At Present

Sl. No.	*Assets*	*Small*		*Marginal*		*Large*		*Total*	
		Q.	*Value*	*Q.*	*Value*	*Q*	*Value*	*Q*	*Value*
1. Land									
	(i) Wet	2.0	27320	4.41	528445	6.7	167305	4.08	8249
	(ii) Dry	1.94	18450	3.47	48667	6.32	110116	4.5	59078
2.	Building	2.3	42120	2.5	58665	3.1	112,845	2.7	14838
3.	Animals	2.1	9900	1.0	22500	2.6	121116	2.7	14838
4.	Agri Imple	3.0	2150	3.4	5818	5.0	28416	4.1	12128
5.	Vehicles	1.6	4818	4.5	12324	2.1	14827	2.4	10988
6.	Jewels	5.3	23585	2.3	43680	12.4	56978	27.5	41414
7.	Furniture	1.1	18195	2.6	4460	2.8	5895	2.7	4083
8.	Others	—	2760	9.8	6158	—	785	—	5500
	Total		149298		730717		618283		171116

Source: Computed from primary data.

Note: Value in Rupees, Quantity in Numbers/acres.

The average land owned by the small farmers was 2.0 acres of wet land and 1.94 acres of dry land at the value of Rs. 27230 and Rs. 52845 respectively. The marginal farmers owned the 4.41 acres of wet land and 3.47 acre of dry land at the value of Rs. 52843 and Rs. 48667 respectively. The large farmers owned 61 acres wet land and 6.32 acres of dry land at the value of Rs. 167305 and Rs. 110116 respectively in the year 2001-02.

At the gross level, the changes in the average asset value was Rs.. .... for small farmers, Rs. .... For marginal farmers and Rs. .... For large farmers. On the whole there is a growth in the asset value due to the inflationary pressure in the economy.

Employment

The details of the employment status of the selected respondents are given in Table 4.8. From the table it is clear that there was difference in the average level of monthly employment per household between the small, marginal and large farmers groups.

The average employment level of the small farmers group was 25 days per month (83.3 per cent) in their own land and 5 days in non-agriculture work (16.7 per cent), the marginal farmers group employed for 24.6 days per month (82 per cent) in their own land and for 5.4 days per month 918 per cent) in non-agriculture work and the large farmers group respondents employed for 27.6 days per month (92 per cent) in their own land and for 2.4 days per month (8 per cent) in non-agriculture work during the year 1993-94.

Table 4.8: Average Monthly Employment Status of the Sample Respondents

Sl. No.	*Farmers*	*Name of the Block 1993-94*											
		Aruppukottai			*Tenkasi*			*Srivaikundam*			*Total*		
		Agri	*N.A.*	*Total*	*Ag.*	*N.A.*	*Total*	*Ag.*	*N.A.*	*Total*	*Ag.*	*N.A.*	*Total*
1.	SF	25	5	30	24	6	30	26	4	30	25	5	30
2.	MF	24	6	30	27	3	30	23	7	30	24.6	5.4	30
3.	LF	28	2	30	28	2	30	27	3	30	27.6	2.4	30
Average		25.6	4.33	30	26.3	3.66	30	25.33	4.66	30	25.7	4.3	30

In the year 2001-02, the average employment of the small farmers group respondent 17.7 days per month (59 per cent) in the agriculture work and for 12.3 days per month (41 per cent) in their agri work. The marginal farmers group respondents employed for 20 days per month (66.7 per cent) in their agriculture work and for 10 days per month (33.3 per cent) in other work and the large farmers groups respondents

Table 4.9: At Present

Sl. No.	Far-mers	Aruppukottai			Tenkasi			Srivaikundam			Total		
		Agri	N.A.	Total	Ag.	N.A.	Total	Ag.	N.A.	Total	Ag.	N.A.	Total
1.	SF	20	10	30	18	12	320	18	15	36	17.7	10	30
2.	MF	22	8	30	20	10	30	18	12	30	20	9	30
3.	LF	21	9	30	22	8	30	4	9	30	21	10.4	30
Average		21	9	30	20	10	30	18	12	30	19.6	10.4	30

Source: Computed from primary data.

Note: Agri-Agriculture, N.A.—Non agriculture, To Total.

employed for 21 days per month (78 per cent) in their agri work and for 9 days per month (22 per cent) in other work.

It is clear that marginal farmers group respondents got the meager level of employment from their own land and higher level of employment from non-agriculture work by small farmers in the sample districts of Tamil Nadu.

Annual Income

Table 4.10: Average Annual Income of the Sample Respondents (1993-94) (in Rs.)

Sl. No.	Name of the Block	Small	Marginal	Large	Total
1.	Aruppukottai				
	(i) Agri work	24762.8	61529.4	159210.5	245502.7
	(ii) Non-Agri work	663	600.0	2160	3393.6
	Total	25396.4	62129.4	161370.5	248896.3
2.	Tenkasi				
	(i) Agri Work	33219.2	70515.3	167301.8	271136.3
	(ii) Non-Agri work	568.0	704.7	2495.0	3677.8
	Total	33787.2	71220.1	169706.8	274714.1
3.	Srivaikudam				
	(i) Agri work	20452.6	75331.5	297002.5	392786.6
	(ii) Non-Agri work	485.1	826.4	2880.0	4191.5
	Total	20937.7	76157.9	299882.5	396978.1
	Gross Total	80121.3	209504.4	630959.8	920588.5
	Average total	26707.1	69835.8	2,10319.9	306862.8

Table 4.11: At Present

1.	Aruppukottai				
	(i) Agri Work	38538.6	65515.6	196406.9	300461.1
	(ii) Non-Agri work	129.2	2585.7	3610.6	7315.5
	Total	39757.8	68001.3	200027.5	30776.6
2.	Tenkasi				
	(i) Agri work	42118.3	76146.1	202355.4	320619.8
	(ii) Non-Agri work	1001.6	2123.7	3987.5	7112.8
	Total	43119.9	78269.8	206342.9	327732.6
3.	Srivaikundam				
	(i) Agri work	27119.3	79876.2	254012.7	361008.2
	(ii) Non Agri work	1106.5	2999.11	39980.4	8086.0
	Total	28225.8	82875.3	257993.1	36904.2
	Average total	37034.5	229146.4	664323.5	1004603.4

Table 4.12: Changes in Average

Sl. No.	*Year*	*Small*	*Marginal*	*Large*	*Total*
1.	1993-94	26707.1	69835.8	210319.9	306862.8
2.	2001-02	37034.5	76382.1	221451.1	334867.8
	Changes	10327.4	6546.3	1113.1	28005.0

Source: Computed from primary data 2001.

Note: Figures within the parenthesis denotes as percentage to the total respondents.

Table 4.11 reveals that the average annual household income was Rs. 26,707.1 for small farmes group respondents family Rs. 69835.8 marginal farmers groups and Rs. 210319.9 for the large farmers group respondents in 1993-94. The average annual household the income of small farmers, marginal farmers and the large farmers were Rs. 37034.5, Rs. 76382.1 and 2,21451.1 respectively in the year 2001-02. The changes in average household of annual income was Rs. 310327.4, for the small farmers Rs. 65466.3 for marginal farmers and for Rs. 11131.2 for the large farmers during the period from 1993-94 and 2001-02. The study found that changes in the marginal farmers annual income was less than the small and large farmers annual income due to the inefficiency and limited input use in the land.

Savings

Table 4.13: Average Annual Household Savings of the Sample Respondents (1993-94) (in Rs.)

Sl. No.	*Block*	*Farmers*			
		Small	*Marginal*	*Large*	*All*
1.	Arupuukottai				
(i)	Coop/Bank	360.5	652.6	1183.1	732.0
(ii)	Money lenders	148.4	201.5	425.2	258.3
(iii)	Relation	—	—	250.0	83.3
	Total	508.9	843.1	1858.3	1073.7
2.	Tenkasi				
(i)	Coop/Bank	396.7	745.9	1212.0	784.8
(ii)	Money lenders	115.1	214.8	385.2	241.7
(ii)	Relation	150.0	155.0	273.0	179.5
	Total	661.8	1076.3	1870.2	1202.7
3.	Srivaikundam				
(i)	Coop-Bank	207.6	811.3	1685.1	931.3
(ii)	Money lenders	117.8	118.5	117.0	117.7
(iii)	Relation	—	200.6	280.6	160.3
	Total	415.4	1130.4	2082.6	1209.4
	Average	528.7	1019.9	1937.0	1161.6

Table 4.13 and 4.14 explain the block wise average annual household savings of the respondents. The average annual household savings of the small farmers, marginal and large farmers was Rs. 528.7, Rs. 1019.9 and Rs. 1937 respectively in 1993-94. It was compared with the savings of

Table 4.14: At Present

1. Aruppukottai				
(i) Coop/Bank	298.2	502.7	968.6	59.1
(ii) Money lender	135.0	195.1	392:5	240.8
(iii) Relationship	433.2	153.6	203.0	118.8
Total	433.2	825.4	1564.1	949.9
2. Tenkasi				
(i) Coop/Bank	203.0	498.5	980.5	560.6
(ii) Money lender	154.2	210.3	200.6	178.1
(iii) Relationship	—	156.3	203.0	118.8
Total	327.2	865.3	1376.3	92.2
3. Srivaikundam				
(i) Coop/Bank	283.1	750.1	1390.3	807.8
(ii) Money lender	110.5	180.4	195.5	162.1
(iii) Relationship	178.2	261.5	276.3	238.6
Total	517.8	1192.0	1862.1	1708.6
Average	440.0	969.9	160.0	156.7

Source: Computed from primary data.

the small, marginal and large farmer groups was Rs. 440, Rs. 969 and 1601.0 respectively in the year 2001-02.

It is clear from the table that the small farmers family had a low level of savings and the greater level of the savings by the marginal and large farmers during the study periods between 1993-94 and 2001-02. The charges in average annual household savings of the small, marginal and large farmers had fallen to the level of Rs. 84.7, Rs. 50.0 and Rs. 336 respectively.

Indebtedness

Table 4.15: Annual Indebtedness of the Respondent (1993-94) (in Rs.)

Sl. No.	*Name of the Block*	*Farmers*			
		Small	*Marginal*	*Large*	*Average*
1.	Aruppukottai				
(i)	Coop/Bank	11640	28300	41800	27246.6
(ii)	Money lender	2600	1900	5300	3266.6
(iii)	Relation	1000	1200	3400	1866.6
	Total	15240	31400	50500	32380.0
2.	Tenkasi				
(i)	Coop/Bank	18580	29600	42200	30126.6
(ii)	Money lenders	2300	2100	5850	3416.6
(ii)	Relationship	800	1350	3150	1766.6
	Total	21680	33050	51200	35310
3.	Srivaikundam				
(i)	Coop/Bank	900	31800	58500	33266.6
(ii)	Money lender	1500	2000	4300	2600
(iii)	Relationship	500	1000	2550	1350
	Total	11500	34800	65350	37216.6
	Average	16140	33083.3	55683.3	104906.6

The main source of debt for the respondents was from the cooperative Banks, money lender and relations etc. As can be seen from Table 4.10 that at the gross level, small farmers have average annual debt Rs. 16140, Rs. 33083 for marginal farmers and Rs. 55683 for large farmers in 1993-94 and it was increased to Rs. 33966 for small, Rs. 52416 for marginal farmers and 74383 for large farmers in 2001-02.

On the whole, the changes in the average annual household income, savings and indebtedness of the sample

Table 4.16: At Present

1. Aruppukottai				
(i) Coop/Bank	25800	44850	68750	46466.6
(ii) Money lender	4200	2500	6000	4233.3
(iii) Relationship	32300	200	400	2766.6
Total	32300	49350	78750	53466.6
2. Tenkasi				
(ii) Coop/Bank	32100	47400	7800	50433.3
(ii) Money lender	4000	3000	6500	4500.0
(iii) Relationship	2000	2500	4000	2833.3
Total	38100	52900	82300	57766.6
3. Srivaikundam				
(i) Coop/Bank	26500	49500	55300	43766.6
(ii) Money lenders	3500	2000	2800	2766.6
(iii) Relationship	1500	5500	62100	49533.3
Average total	33966	52416	74383	53586.6
Changes	+17826	+19333	18700	18620

Source: Computed from primary data.

respondent revealed that the economics status of the sample farmers have been decreased to a great extend during the study periods from 1994-95 to 2001-02 in South Tamil Nadu.

IMPACT OF AGRICULTURAL ENVIRONMENT

Area Cultivated by Farmers

In order to find out the area used for agriculture by the different category of farmers during the different periods of time is selected district of Tamil Nadu, the data collected from the farmers about the area of land cultivated and uncultivated. The results are explained in the following tables.

Table 4.17: Average Area Cultivated by the Respondents in Arupukaottai Block (1993-94)

(in acres)

Sl. No.	*Land Particulars*	*Wet Land*	*Dry land*	*Total*
1.	Own land	8.341	2.031	10.372
2.	Rent land	4.117	3.119	7.336
	Total	12.458	5.150	17.708
3.	Uncultivated land	1.101	0.736	1.837

Table 4.18: At present

S. No.		*Wet*	*Dry*	*Total*	*Changes*
1.	Own land	8.15	10.115	2.003	-0.254
2.	Rent land	2.197	6.200	2.197	-1.136
	Total	4.200	16.318	4.200	-1.380
3.	Uncultivated Land	0.814	2.750	0.814	+0.913

Source: Computed from primary data.

Table 4.19: Average Area Cultivated by the Respondents in Tenkasi Block (1993-94)

(in acres)

Sl. No.	*Land Particulars*	*Wet Land*	*Dry land*	*Total*
1.	Own	9.521	2.175	11.696
2.	Rent	5.63	2.040	7.670
	Total	15.151	4.215	19.366
3.	Uncultivated land	0.980	0.530	1.510

Table 4.20: At Present

Sl. No.	*Land Particulars*	*Wet*	*Dry*	*Total*	*Changes*
1.	Own	9.072	2.075	11.147	-0.549
2.	Rent	4.190	2.130	6.020	-1.650
3.	Uncultivated land	1.330	0.780	2,100	+0.600
	Total	13.262	4.205	17.167	+0.600

Source: Computed form primary data.

Table 4.21: Average Area Cultivated by the Respondents in Sri Vaikundam block (1993-94)

(in acres)

Sl. No.	*Land Particulars*	*Wet Land*	*Dry land*	*Total*
1.	Own land	8.112	2.510	10.622
2.	Rented	5.730	4.130	9.866
	Total	13.842	6.646	20.488
3.	Uncultivated	1.530	0.910	2.440

Table 4.22: At Present

Sl. No.	*Land Particulars*	*Wet*	*Dry*	*Total*	*Changes*
1.	Own land	8.003	1.970	9.973	-0.649
2.	Rent	4.641	3.854	8.495	1.371
3.	Total	12.644	5.824	18.468	-2.020
	Uncultivated	1.922	1.170	3.092	+0.625

Source: Computed from primary data.

Table 4.23: Average Area Cultivated by the Respondent in Study District (1993-94)

(in acres)

S. No	*Land Particulars*	*Aruppukottai*	*Tenkasi*	*Srivaukundam*	*Total*
1.	Own	10.372	11.696	10.622	10.879
2.	Rented	7.336	7.670	9.866	8.289
	Total	17.708	19.366	20.488	19.184
3.	Uncultivated	1.837	1.262	2.440	5.539

Table 4.24: (2000-01)

1.	Own	10.188	11.147	9.973	10.413
2.	Rent	6.200	6.020	8.495	6.905
	Total	16.318	17.167	18.468	17.318
3.	Uncultivated	2.750	2.100	3.092	7.952
	Changes				
(i)	Cultivated	-1.380	-2.299	-2.020	-10.866
(ii)	Uncultivated	+0.913	+0.848	+0.652	0.804

Source: Computed from primary data.

The average area cultivated by the respondent is explained in Table 4.23. It is clear that the average area cultivated with own land was 17.708 acre in Aruppukottai block 19.366 acre in Tenkasi and 20.488 acre in Srivilliputtur block in the year 1993-94 and it has decreased to 16.318 acre in Aruppukottai block, 17.167 acres in Tenkasi block and 18.468 acre in Srivakundam block in the year 2001-02.

From the table, few facts could be inferred that the uncultivable land has increased from 1.837 acre to 2.750 acre in Aruppukottai block, 1.262 acre to 2.100 acre in Tenkasi block and 2.440 acre to 3.092 acre in Srivaikundam block during the period 1993-94 and 2001-02. It is concluded that the uncultivable land had increased from 5.539 are to 7.952 acre during the study period in the study districts.

Irrigation

Irrigation is one of the important factor which is therefore the agriculture development and the environmental

Table 4.25: Average—Irrigation by the Various Sources in Aruppukottai Block

(Area in acre)

Sl. No.	*Farmers*	*Bore well*	*Well*	*Canal/Tank*	*River*	*Total*
1.	Small	0.500	1.398	0.426	0.416	2.092
2.	Marginal	1.387	2.710	0.510	0.813	5.420
3.	Large	1.454	2.516	0.751	1.361	6.082
	All	1.113	2.208	0.562	0.863	4.531
	Percentage	22.5	46.7	11.4	15.3	100.0
			At Present			
1.	Small	0.334	1.387	0.325	0.303	2.349
2.	Marginal	1.145	2.691	0.745	0.749	5.330
3.	Large	1.001	2.334	0.851	1.282	5.478
	All	0.826	2.137	0.643	0.778	4.385
	Percentage	18.8	48.7	14.7	17.8	100.0

Source: Computed from primary data.

degradation. Due to the changes in the environmental condition, the irrigation availability and uses have been change from time to time and place to place. The data collected regarding irrigation from the sample respondents are analysed in Tables 4.25, 4.26, 4.27 and 4.28.

Table 4.26: Average—Irrigation by the Various Sources in Tenkasi Block

(Area in acre)

Sl. No.	*Sources*	*Bore well*	*Well*	*Canal*	*River*	*Total*
			1993-94			
1.	Small	0.311	0.398	0.317	1.387	2.409
2.	Marginal	1.014	0.416	0.897	2.863	5.190
3.	Large	0.457	0.345	1.991	3.953	6.746
	Average	0.594	0.386	1.068	2.734	4.781
	Percentage	12.4	8.1	22.3	57.2	100.0
			At Present			
1.	Small	0.301	0.284	0.296	1.289	2.170
2.	Marginal	1.084	0.452	0.743	2.512	4.791
3.	Large	0.432	0.139	1.886	3.824	6.281
	Average	0.605	0.291	0.975	2.541	4.414
	Percentage	13.7	6.59	22.0	57.4	100.0

Source: Computed from primary data.

Table 4.27: Average—Irrigated Land by the Various Sources in Srivaikundam Block

(Area in acre)

Sl. No.	*Sources*	*Bore well*	*Well*	*Canal*	*River*	*Total*
1.	Small	1.723	2.35	0.316	1.118	5.507
2.	Marginal	1.123	0.314	1.114	2.987	5.538
3.	Large	1.850	1.135	0.840	3.913`	7.738
	Average	1.565	1.266	0.756	2.672	6.261
	Percentage	24.9	20.2	12.2	42.7	100.0

		At present				
1.	Small	1.914	2.001	0.273	1.007	5.12
2.	Marginal	1.100	0.321	1.104	2.522	5.047
3.	Large	1.767	1.381	0.826	3.713	7.687
	Average	1.593	1.234	0.736	2.414	5.953
	Percentage	26.7	20.5	12.4	40.4	100.0

Source: Computed from primary data.

Table 4.28: Block-wise Average—irrigated land

(Area in acre)

Sl. No.	*Farmers*	*Aruppukottai*	*Tenkasi*	*Srivaikundam*	*All*	*Changes*
1.	Small	2.092	2.109	1.507	1.872	
2.	Marginal	4.420	5.190	5.538	5.383	
3.	Large	6.082	6.746	7.738	6.855	
	Average	4.531	4.681	4.927	4.703	
		At present changes				
1.	Small	2.349	2.170	2.195	2.238	0.366
2.	Marginal	5.330	4.791	5.047	5.056	0.327
3.	Large	5.478	6.281	7.687	6.482	3.730
	Average	4.385	4.414	4.976	4.592	1.474

Source: Computed from primary data.

The ground water is the major soruce of irrigation in all study districts. In Aruppukottai block, the average irrigated land was 6.624 acre by the ground water in 1993-94 and it was decreased to 6.412 acre in 2001-02 i.e. 0.212 acre decreased for the ground water sources. In Tenkasi block the average irrigated land was 8.199 acre by the river base in 1993-94 and it was decreased to 7.625 acre in 2001-02 i.e. 0.574 acre decreased for the river base sources. In Srivaikundam block, the average land irrigated was 8,081 acre by the source of river base in 1993-94 and it was decreased to 7.242 acre 2001-02 i.e. 0.776 acre decreased for the source of the river base.

It is inferred that the average land irrigated was 13.594 acre in Aruppukottai block during the year 1993-94 and it was decreased to 13.157 acre in 2001-02 and the average irrigated land was 12.783 acre in Srivaikundam block during the year 1993-94 and it was decreased to 17.929 acre in 2001-02.

Yield, Cropping Pattern and Cost of Cultivation Per Acre

Table 4.29: Cropping Pattern and Yield Per Acre in Aruppukottai Block

		1993-94	*2001-02*	
Sl. No.	*Crop*	*Yield per acre (kg)*	*Yield per acre (kg)*	*Changes*
1.	Paddy	2520	2150	-370
2.	Cholan	2110	1780	-430
3.	Ragi	750	600	-245
4.	Gingelly	1150	1250	-110
5.	Groundnut	1120	990	-130
6.	Sugar	4.75	4.12	-.63

Source: Computed from primary data.

Table 4.30: Yield per acre in Tenkasi Block

		1993-94	*2001-02*	
Sl. No.	*Crop*	*Yield (per acre in kg)*	*Yield (per acre in kg)*	*Changes*
1.	Paddy	2840	2235	-615
2.	Cholam	2000	1870	-130
3.	Ragi	800	770	-30
4.	Pulses	720	650	-70
5.	Cotton	640	650	-40
6.	Groundnut	1200	600	-150
7.	Sugar	3.95	1050	-59

Source: Computed from primary data.

Table 4.31: Cropping Pattern and Yield per acre in Srivaikundam Block

		1993-94	*2001-02*	
Sl. No.	*Crop*	*Yield per acre (kg)*	*Yield per acre (kg)*	*Changes*
1.	Paddy	2475	2220	-255
2.	Gingelly	1280	1170	-110
3.	Groundnut	1310	1216	-94
4.	Cotton	690	645	-95
5.	Sugar (Tonnes)	4.00	3.45	-25
6.	Chillis	360	345	-25
7.	Plantain	650	600	-50

Source: Computed from primary data.

Table 4.29 reveals that average yield per acre in Aruppukottai block of Virudhunagar district was 2520 kg/per acre for the paddy crop in 1993-94 it was decreased to 2150 kg/per acre at present. The yield of cholam, ragi, groundnut and sugar, was 210 kg, 750 kg, 1120 kg. 4.75 kg. respectively in 1993-94 and it was decreased to 1780, 600, 990, and 4.12 kilograms in 2001-02 except the gingelly crop it was increased from 1150 kg. per acre to 1260 kg. per acre during the period (1993-94 and 2001-02) in Aruppukottai block.

The average yield per acre in Tenkasi block of Tirunelveli district was decreased for all crops such as 615 kg for paddy, 130 kgs for cholam, 30 kgs for ragi, 70 kgs for pulses, 40 kgs for cotton, 150 kgs for groundnut and 59 kgs for cholam.

Similarly, the average yield per acre was also decreased as 255 kgs for paddy, 110 kgs for gingelly, 94 kgs for groundnut, 95 kgs for cotton, 2.5 tonnes for sugarcane and 25 kgs. for chilies and 50 kgs for plantation per acre of cultivation in Tuticorin district of Tamil Nadu.

In these three blocks, the changes in paddy crop yield per acre is highly decreased as 370 kgs in Arpukottai block, 615 in Tenkasi block and 255 kgs is Srivaikundam block from 1993-94 and 2001-02.

There is an increase in the average cost of cultivation for all activities and for all crops in the study district. Due to the inflationary pressure, increase in the cost of living and price rise, the cost of cultivation automatically increased in the agricultural yield. The changes in yield per acre, cropping pattern, average cost of cultivation (1993-94), average cost of cultivation (2001-02) and changes in the average cost of cultivation are explained in Tables 4.30, 4.31, 4.33 and 4.34 respectively.

Use of Chemicals

Table 4.35 explains the average changes of fertilisers and pesticides used in cultivable land in study area. It is normally increased year by year i.e., 1993-94 and 2001-02. The changes of quantity of fertilizer use on paddy, groundnut, cotton, pulses, gingelly, maize, ragi, sugar, plantain, vegetables and chilies was 38 kg, 56 kg, 48kg, 27 kg, 26 kg, 33 kg, 15 kg, 20 kg, 11 kg, and 55 kg, respectively. The changes in the cost of fertiliser was Rs. 446, Rs. 448, Rs. 110 Rs. 206, Rs. 115, Rs. 545, Rs. 85, Rs. 70, Rs. 44 and Rs. 825 respectively during the period from 1993-94 to 2001-02.

At the same time the changes in the quantity of pesticide on paddy, groundnut pulses, gingelly, ragi, sugar, plantain, vegetables, and chilies was 0.45 liter, 0.4 litre, 0.3 litre, .57 litre, 4 litre, 0.8 litre, 1 litre, 0.3 litre and 0.4 litre respectively. The changes in the value of pesticides was Rs. 415, Rs. 260, Rs. 1160 Rs. 610, Res. 450, Rs. 260, Rs. 750, Rs. 1120 and Rs. 585 respectively available during the period 1993-94 and 2001-01.

Option of the Farmers

The field survey covered the opinion of the farmers regarding the reasons for decreasing the cultivated land, reasons for changes in the source of irrigation, causes for the changes in the cropping pattern, reasons for decreasing the yield crop, control measures for the use of chemicals in land, steps taken by the Government and other agency to reduce the environment degradation, etc.

Table 4.32: Average Cost of Cultivation in 1993-94 (cost/per acre)

Sl. No.	*Sources*	*Paddy*	*Groundnut*	*Cotton*	*Pulses*	*Chilies*	*Ragi*	*Plantain*	*Sugar*	*Veg.*
1.	Ploughing	1500	440	1100	800	500	700	1000	800	650
2.	Seeding	250	250	340	150	230	145	185	200	190
3.	Realignment of Boundaries	120	110	—	150	210	175	250	195	210
4.	Cost of Transplantation	550	—	—	—	—	—	440	400	290
5.	Cost of Fertiliser	650	390	450	210	—	—	500	600	550
6.	Seeding	175	185	755	110	120	100	210	320	110
7.	Pesticides	360	190	420	250	200	240	340	180	1450
8.	Harvesting	475	440	680	310	310	290	450	1100	490
	Total	4030	2005	3745	1770	1570	1650	3080	3795	3940

Source: Computed from primary data.

Table 4.33: Average Cost of Cultivation by the Respondents (cost/per acre) (Rs.)

Sl. No.	*Sources*	*Paddy*	*Groundnut*	*Cotton*	*Pulses*	*Chillies*	*Ragi*	*Plantain*	*Vegetables*	*Sugar*
1.	Ploughing	1700	700	1510	1000	600	850	1200	800	1400
2.	Seeding	280	350	620	240	250	250	310	300	310
3.	Realignment of Boundaries	195	275	—	215	—	—	375	410	280
4.	Cost of Transplantation	540	—	—	—	—	—	—	800	590
5.	Cost of fertiliser	870	660	815	—	—	—	620	800	750
6.	Seedling cost	390	450	1300	175	190	220	340	200	1440
7.	Pesticides	450	300	750	360	280	275	550	2100	460
8.	Harvesting	880	600	360	280	620	380	560	630	1800
	Total	5405	3335	5855	2470	2455	2315	4505	5605	7030

Table 4.34: Changes in Average Cost of Cultivation

Sl. No.	Sources	Paddy	Groundnut	Cotton	Pulses	Chillies	Ragi	Sugar	Plantain	Vegetables
1.	Ploughing	+200	+260	+410	+200	100	150	600	200	150
2.	Seeding	80	+100	+280	+90	120	105	110	130	170
3.	Realignment bounddaring	70	—	—	—	—	—	190	110	190
4.	Cost of Transplantation	90	—	—	—	—	—	350	70	250
5.	Cost of fertilisers	+220	+270	+365	—	—	—	350	70	250
6.	Weeding cost	+215	+205	+545	+65	+70	100	120	130	90
7.	Pesticides	+90	+260	+330	+110	+180	75	240	210	650
8.	Harvesting	+405	+160	+180	+170	+310	+70	700	110	140
	Total	1370	1420	2110	700	985	665	3395	1085	1790

Source: Computed from primary data.

Table 4.35: Average use of Fertiliser and Pesticides in Cultivable land Study Area

Sl. No.	Crop	1993-94				At Present				Changes			
		Fertilizer		Pesticides		Fertilizer		Pesticides		Fertilizer		Pesticides	
		Qty.	Value	Qty	Value	Qty	Value	Qty	Value	Qt.	Value	Qty	Value
1.	Paddy	74	296	1.53	1635	112	742	1.98	2050	+38	+446	+0.45	+415
2.	Ground	65	238	2.2	1300	121	686	2.6	2560	+56	+448	+0.4	+260
3.	Cotton	102	395	4.5	4200	150	505	3.2	5500	+48	110	+1.3	+1300
4.	Pulses	36	174	1	680	63	280	1.3	1840	+27	+206	+.3	+1160
5.	Maize	12	126	—	—	23	160	—	—	+11	+34	—	—
6.	Ragi	107	350	1.2	1000	140	895	1.6	1450	+33	+545	+0.4	+450
7.	Sugars	185	475	1	800	200	510	1.8	1060	+15	+85	+.8	+260
8.	Plantain	90	210	1	705	110	280	2	1500	+20	+70	1	+750
9.	Vegetables	74	221	2.7	1880	85	265	3.6	3000	+11	+44	+3	+1120
10.	Chillies	235	575	1.47	815	290	1400	1.85	1750	+55	+825	+0.4	+585

Sources: Computed from primary data, 2001.

Table 4.36: Opinion of the Respondents Regarding Reasons for Decreasing Cultivated Land

Sl. No.	*Reasons*	*No. of Respondents*			
		Aruppu-kottai	*Ten-kasi*	*Srivikun-dam*	*Total*
1.	Land Degradation	73	52	71	196 (43.5)
2.	Improper maintenance	14	23	12	49 (10.7)
3.	Integrated cultivation	22	25	32	79 (17.7)
4.	Fools	10	21	15	46 (10.3)
5.	Low yield	16	18	14	48 (10.6)
6.	Migration	15	11	6	32 (7.2)
	Total	150	150	150	450(100.0)

Source: Computed from primary data, 2001.

Note: Figures within the parenthesis denotes the percentages.

It reveals that 43.5 per cent (196 respondents) known the land degradation is the important reasons for increasing the uncultivated land in study area. The remaining 17.7 per cent (79 respondents) of respondents, 10.7 per cents (48 respondents) 10.3 per cent (46 respondents) 7.2 per cent (32 respondents) viewed integrated cultivation, maintenance of the land, low yield in land and migration of the farmers from the one place to other place respectively.

Thus, land degradation and Integrated cultivation (17.7 per cent) are the major reasons for the addition in the uncultivated land in the study area during the period from 1993-94 to 2001-02.

The study found that only 14.0 per cent of the respondent understand the land capacity is the major reason for the changes in the sources of irrigation. The remaining respondents accepted the but low ground water, low rainfall, and low tank irrigation were the major reasons for the changes in the source of irrigation.

It observed from the table that 151 respondents (33.56 per cent) opinion about the reasons for the changes in the

Table 4.37: Reasons for the Changes in the Sources of Irrigation

Sl. No.	*Sources*	*No. of Respondents*			
		Aruppu-kottai	*Ten-kasi*	*Srivikun-dam*	*Total*
1.	Low ground water	41	53	57	151 (33.56)
2.	Low Tank Irrigation	33	28	30	91 (20.22)
3.	Depend upon the land capacity	21	20	22	63 (14.00)
	Total	150	150	150	450 (100.00)

Source: Computed from primary data 2001.

Note: Figures within the parenthesis denotes percentages.

source of cultivation as low ground water potential in the study area during the period from 1993-94 to 2001-02.

Table 4.38: Details about the Causes for in the Changes in the Cropping Pattern

Sl. No.	*Reasons*	*No. of Respondents*			
		Aruppu-kottai	*Ten-kasi*	*Srivikun-dam*	*Total*
1.	Soil protection	39 (26.0)	48 (32.0)	45 (30.0)	132 (29.33)
2.	High yielding for other crop	59 (39.3)	55 (36.7)	59 (39.3)	173 (38.44)
3.	Seasonal crop Cultivation	52 (34.7)	47 (31.3)	46 (30.7)	145 (32.22)
	Total	150 (100.00)	150 (100.00)	150 (100.00)	450(100.00)

Source: Computed from primary data.

Note: Figures within the parenthesis denotes percentage.

As can be seen from Table, the higher percentage of 38.44 respondents opined that the high yielding for other crop cultivation is the cause for changes in the cropping pattern in study district. The opinion of 32.23 per cent respondents was the seasonal crop cultivation and soil protection

(29.33 per cent) is the main causes for changes in the cropping pattern.

It is clear that 173 respondent opinion is high yielding other crops which is the major changes in the cropping pattern of the sample blocks of the study districts during the period 1993-94 to 2001-02.

Table 4.39: Respondents Opinion about the Reason for Decreasing the Yield Crop

Sl. No.	*Reasons*	*No. of Respondents*			
		Aruppu-kottai	*Ten-kasi*	*Srivaikun-dam*	*Total*
1.	Integrated crop	11	14	12	37 (8.22)
2.	Land Degradation	12	16	13	41 (9.11)
3.	Solid contamination	185	10	15	40 (8.89)
4.	Dry land	20	8	14	42 (9.33)
5.	Solid Erosion	18	35	31	84 (18.67)
6.	Water scarcity	31	17	17	65 (14.44)
7.	Rainfall failure	33	15	16	54 (12.00)
8.	Running water	8	26	17	51 (11.34)
9.	Common property	7	5	8	20 (4.44)
10.	Urbanisation	5	4	7	16 (3.56)
	Total	150	150	150	450

Source: Computed from primary data.

Note: Figures within the parenthesis denotes percentages.

The table reveals that the respondents opinion about the decreasing the yield crop are 37 respondents for integrated cultivation for land degradation, 41 respondents for 40 respondents for salt contamination, dry land, 42 respondents for 84 soil erosion, 65 respondents for water scarcity for 54 respondents for rainfall failure, 51 respondents for running water, 20 respondents for common property resources, 16 respondents for urbanisation.

The study found that 18.67 per cent of respondents (84. respondents) accepted the soil erosion is the cause for low yield in cultivation in the three blocks of the districts, during the period from 1993-94 to 2001-02.

Regarding the opinion about the control measurement for the use of chemical fertilizer in the cultivable land in the study area, 53 respondents (11.78 percentages) are using the pesticides in the cultivable land and 397 respondents (88.22 per cent) are not using any pesticides and chemicals in the cultivable land.

Table 4.40: Opinion about the Control Measures for the Use of Chemical Fertiliser in Land

Sl. No.	*Opinion*	*No. of the Block*			
		Aruppu-kottai	*Tenkasi*	*Srivaikundam*	*Total*
(i)	Yes	24 (16.0)	12	17	53 (11.78)
(ii)	No.	126 (84.0)	138 (92.0)	133 (88.67)	397 (88.22)
	Total	150 (100.00)	150 (100.00)	150 (100.00)	450 (100.00)
	If 'Yes' Effort				
(i)	Changes of cultivation	8 (33.33)	7 (58.33)	3 (17.64)	18 (33.96)
(ii)	Water resource	11 (45.83)	3 (25.00)	10 (58.83)	24 (45.29)
(iii)	Soil erosion control measures	5 (20.83)	2 (16.67)	4 (23.53)	11 (20.75)
	Total	24 (100.00)	12 (100.00)	17 (100.00)	53 (100.00)
	If 'No' Alter-native Idea				
(i)	Agri work in other land	44 (34.92)	49 (35.11)	53 (39.85)	146 (35.77)
(ii)	Non-agri work	47 (37.30)	58 (42.62)	37 (27.82)	142 (35.77)
(iii)	Alternative	35 (27.78)	31 (21.77)	43 (32.33)	109 (27.45)
	Total	126 (100.00)	138 (100.00)	133 (100.00)	397 (100.00)

Source: Computed from primary data.

Note: Figures within the parenthesis denotes the percentages.

45.29 per cent of respondents are taking effort on water resource management, 33.96 percentage of respondents are involving in the change of cultivation and 20.75 percentage of respondents accepted that ineffective soil erosion control measure due to the low use of chemical fertiliser in the land.

In order to improve the agricultural land, the opinion survey revealed that the 397 (88.72 percentage) respondents are not taking any effort for controlling the use of chemical fertilizer due to low technological knowledge in agricultural work in the study area. Of the 397 respondents, 146 respondents (36.78 per cent) suggested the agriculture work in other land, 142 respondents (35.77 per cent) for non-agricultural work and 109 respondents (27.45 per cent) for the migration from one place to other place.

Table 4.41: Details about the assistance from the Government and other agency for controlling the degradation.

Sl. No.	*Assistance*	*No. of Respondents*			
		Aruppukottai	*Tenkasi*	*Srivaikundam*	*Total*
1.	Training	25 (22.32)	23 (21.90)	31 (21.84)	79(22.00)
2.	Fertilizers	169 (23.21)	19 (18.00)	29 (27.46)	84(23.40)
3.	Subsiding for free equipment	18 (16.07)	25 (23.81)	15 (10.56)	58(16.16)
4.	Soil Test	43 (38.40)	38 (36.19)	57 (40.14)	138(38.44)
	Total	250 (100.00)	105 (100.00)	132 (100.00)	359 (100.00)

Source: Computed from primary data.

Note: Figures within the parenthesis denotes percentage.

Table 4.41 gives the details about the assistance from the Government and other agency for controlling land degradation received during the period from 1993-94 to 2001-02. The 38.44 percentage of respondents involved in soil test by the Government, 22 percentage of the respondents undergone the training from the NGO's for the improvement of cultivation and 23.40 per cent of respondents purchase fertilizer and pesticides at subsidy rate from the Department of the Agriculture and Engineering and 16.16 per cent of respondent bought the free equipment bought from voluntary agencies in study districts.

Thus, 138 respondents (38.44) involved in soil testing conducted by the Soil Test Research Centre in study districts.

PROBLEMS REGARDING ENVIRONMENT DEGRADATION AND AGRICULTURAL DEVELOPMENT IN THE STUDY AREA

The general problems regarding environment degradation in agriculture sector of the study districts as follows:

1. Soil is one of the major inputs for agricultural development. The level of knowledge in keeping the soil health is the major constraints and continuous soil erosion levels due to removal of top soil.

2. In the irrigated area of Srivilliputtur and Rajapalayam taluks of Virudunagar district, there is alkaline problem of soils which affects the yield of rice, cotton, chilies and sugarcane.

3. Parodied non-application of organic manure is an another contraption. This is due to the reduced population of livestock in village because of their maintenance cost, rearing the mulch animals make the land suspitiable for soil erosion and ultimately the soil will be unsuitable for cultivation. This is mainly due to urbanisation, industrialisation, increased cost of cultivation and increased demand for agricultural labour.

4. During the recent past, due to increase in the cost of cultivation of food crops, the farmers are switching over dry land areas to perennial crops. Because of the increased demand of agricultural labour, the farmers themselves are cultivating the

lands and seeking jobs in the nearby industries like matches and fire works.

5. Climate change is a serious public concern. Pollution and rapid deforestation are the prime factors leading to climate change. This leads to changes in main pattern and distribution and ultimately in the crop productivity. Frequent alterations in rainfall pattern especially during the east monsoon period.

6. While comparing the extension activities of the past decades to the present one, vast changes have taken place in transfer of technologies and the constraints have been comparatively reduced the poor economic condition of the dry land farmers leads to the non-ADP.

7. Another problem is the lack of plant protection knowledge in the language of pesticides for the crops of cotton, chillies, paddy etc. Lack of motivation and technical knowledge in the adoption of latest technologies in crop production as well as protection of the crops is the main problem in the study areas.

8. High cost of seeds and non-availability of quality seeds especially in cotton reduces the crop yields in the backward regions of Tamil Nadu. Unawareness of the farmers about the seed and high yield production technologies, lack of awareness about the importance of organic manure can create the soil problems.

9. Lack of net work for getting remunerative prices for farm produce like maize and rice discouraged the farmers to continue the agriculture cultivation in the study areas.

10. Lack of suitable crop varieties to withstand the changing advance weather condition of rain-humming temperature etc. affect the profitable yield position in agriculture.

11. There is no vast difference in yield between traditional varieties and hybrids of rice, this will promote the non adoption technology in the backward regions of Tamil Nadu.

12. Establishment of browned castled seedlings under unfavourable conditions like sandy soils, rains and lack of knowledge in special seedlings for use in manual and mechanical transplant are some problems in the study districts. Lack of nutrient management with reference to soil fertility status in the backward region due is increasing to the illiteracy problems.

13. The farmers in the backward regions mostly follow the non-adoption of crop rotation, which will decorate the productivity of the land.

14. The continuous and indiscriminate use of plant protection chemicals, fertilizer lead to the development of resistance to pass and disease pathogens and destruction of predators leading to human hazards and environment pollution. Indiscriminate use of chemicals, pesticides etc. by other means causing unbalance in the natural—preset—pre data systems and eco-system.

15. The study found that there is another problem of limited availability of indigenous implements suitable for seed programme.

16. Lack of quality and quantity seeds in time, vagaries monsoon, animal wastage, country pollution to soil, water and atmosphere, lack of maintenance of irrigation tanks, canals etc. are some other problems in agricultural sector of the study districts.

5

SUMMARY AND CONCLUSIONS

The present chapter explains the major findings of the analysis of the Environment Degradation and Poverty in Backward Region of south Tamil Nadu during period 1985-86 to 1994-95 and findings to the cross section analysis of the impact of environmental degradation in agriculture and alleviating the rural poverty among the farmers and also presented. A few suggestions are offered for the future Policy decisions on the basis of the finding of the study.

SUMMARY

The causes of environmental degradation in India, can be attributed to rapid growth of population. Indian has approximately 18 per cent of world population but only 2 per cent of the geographical area. The application of medical knowledge and social care has lowered the death rate while the birth rate, remaining fairly constant. In the Stockholm Conference on Environment,(1975) the Prime Minister of India Smt. Indira Gandhi has said that poverty is a great pollutant. Twenty years later in 1992 World Bank stated that 'poor are the agents and victims of environment degradation'. The poor become agents of environment degradation when they are victims of it.

The poverty that national debt creates in these countries cannot be calculated nor can it be separated from any initiatives to improve the environment. The poor in urban and rural areas who are deprived of access to adequate housing, water and sewage facilities are caught in a vicious circle of poverty and environmental degradation. According to the latest estimates, the earth's total world water reserves approximately 1,400 million kms of which fresh water amounts to 40 million kilometers(3 or 2.5 per cent).Recent to a report conclude of square kilometers subject to shifting cultivation by hundreds of millions of farmers in Asia, Africa or Latin America the period of fallow has dropped to two or more or three years, and no longer allows the soil to recover its fertility. Yields fall, the farmers gets poorer and the young leave the land. The degraded soil which no longer even has time to rebuild thin plain. The cover is abandoned erosion causes further damage for once the degradation process starts, its tends to accelerate rapidly.

The area under barren and uncultivable land is generally unsuitable for agriculture, either because of the rain in Gujarat, and the weed infected and ravine land in Madhya Pradesh. Recently the area under non-agricultural uses has increased due to the increases development activities such as housing, transport system, irrigation etc. Soil is the non-renewable natural resources which supports use on earth. Excessive soil erosion with consequent high rate of sedimentation in the reservoirs and decreases fertility has become serious environmental problems with disasters economic consequences.

Environmental problems center of human activities which can adversely affect the atmosphere, oceans and land and cover global, national and local concern, ranging from global warming and zone depletion to degradation and soil erosion, contamination of fresh water resources and urban pollution. Many developing countries are concerned about the issues such as soil erosion, water pollution, urban air pollution, and desertification, which impinge on the relationship between; poverty and environmental degradation. Rapid population growth places enormous pressure on all aspect of the environment and combined with deforestation, land degradation and soil erosion, is causing increase in the numbers of these living in extreme poverty. An attempt has been made to analyse the impact of environment degradation on rural poverty in backward regions of Tamil Nadu.

The specific objectives of the present study are (i) to study the impact of land degradation at macro level on net area sown and yield rate of major crops during 1985-86 to 1994-95 in Tamil Nadu (ii) to find out the relation between land and water resource degradation and the occupational structure, employment, income and poverty level of the farmers in the south Tamil Nadu are and (iii) to suggest the proper land and water resource management policies to enahance the income of the farmers in their study area.

The present study used the primary as well as secondary data. Secondary data were used to analyse the regional level environment degradation over a period of time (1984-85-1994-95). Census data from agricultural department, satellite in imageries, topo-sheets of survey of India were analysed cartographically, graphically and statistically to arrive at conclusion. The Geographical Information System were used to classify land capacity. Later, present land use were compared with the proposed land use and occupational planning for backward region.

The south Tamil Nadu is selected as the study area based on physical, demographically, occupational and socio-economic and land related variables. Three districts were selected in the study region. The study districts are (i) Virudunagar district, hilly and plain areas without perennial river (ii) Tirunelveli District with Tamirabarani river and hilly areas, and (iii) Tuticorin District, Industrially developed and coastal area. Through multistage sampling method, three villages were selected as representative villages from each district.

A sample of 150 farmers (small, marginal, large) from the three sample villages (one village panchayat in each district) were randomly selected with the help of verifying land holders. Those landholders having 2.5 acres and below 2.5 acres are considered as small farmers, those land holders having 2.5 to 5.0 acres are considered as marginal farmers and those land holders having 5.0 acres and above are considered as large farmers. A total of 450 farmers were interviewed with a protested questionnaire and the primary data on various aspects were collected during the year 2000-2001. Discussion was made with the farmers in order to identify the reasons for degraded lands and comparison was analysed between the period from 1993-94 and 2000-2001 in south Tamil Nadu.

Thereafter, appropriate tables were prepared keeping in view the specific objectives of the study for analyzing the data with the application of statistical tools. Simple average and tabular analysis were used to analyse the data.

Statistical techniques and before (1993-94) and after (1999-2000) technique and comparative analysis were also used to study the environmental degradation and poverty in backward region of south Tamil Nadu.

FINDINGS

Tamil Nadu secured the first rank in South zone level. In the consumption of fertilizer (128.81 kgs for cropped area, 124.48 kgs for Andhra Pradesh) secured the second for applying the fertilizer in the cropped land.

The mean household income of those below the poverty line is Rs. 1,591 per annum, which is only 33 per cent of the overall per capita income of Rs 4,485 for Rural India.

However, the intensity of poverty is highest among the households classified to the lower segment below the poverty line with a Sen Index of 0.63 and FGT of 0.33, the highest for any category of population group. These indices are 0.22 and 0.44 in the upper segment below the poverty line category of village development are related with poverty. Less developed villages have higher HCR and also a higher Sen Index.

The poverty line for Rural India as a whole is Rs, 2,444 per capita per year. The percentage of the population below the poverty line is estimated to be 39 (in 1994). Poverty is highest in Orissa (55 per cent), West Bengal (51 per cent) and Himachal Pradesh (45 per cent). The incidence of poverty is low in Andhra Pradesh, Haryana, Punjab, and Kerala.

The mean household income of the poor has worked out to be Rs. 1,591 per annum. The HCR among the less that

Rs. 20,000 category is 69 per cent, and in the Rs, 20,001-40,000 category is 13 per cent. The HCR declines substantially as landholding size increases. The HCR is only 16 per cent among STs, the lowest is 27 per cent among Christians and both literate groups. The incidence of poverty is highest among both the lower and upper and segment below poverty line groups.

On the basis of nine-fold land use classification the land use statistics are available for roughly 305 million hectares of the total geographic area, which accounts for 93% of the total land.

About 22 million hectare are occupied by the housing industry and for other non-agricultural uses, 19.5 million hectare are snow bound and remote, leaving only 264 million, hectare for agricultural, forestry, pasture and other biomass production. The data shows that land use in the country, over the last five decades, has undergone drastic change,. Land under agriculture has almost doubled, forest cover has dwindled to less than half, large tracts of fertile agriculture and forest land have been diverted for urbanization and settlements. Deforestation contributes to loss of precious top soil which amount to about 35 per cent of the global sediment load going to ocean even though water flowing through out river is only about five per cent of the flow of rivers in the world.

The data shows that the increase of net area from 118.7 million hectare to 142.2 million hectare, gross cropped area from 131.9 million hectare to 186.4 million hectare and food grains production from 50.8 million tones to 119.5 million tones during 1950-51 and 1993-94. But the new technology has not been intensively adopted throughout the country by taking the overall ecological conditions of the different regions.

The waste land in India is due to non-forest degraded area and forest area. In addition to this, some places have other type of waste land, i.e. degradation and high use of chemical application. Out of 1295.74 thousand square kilometers non-forest degraded area, the waste land in India are 358.89 thousand square kilometer in 1995-96.

The soil erosion through solidity, water logging, erosion wise hand increase from 9.4 m.h. to 11.3 m.h. to 141.5 m.h. to 171.2 m.h. during the period from 1985-86 to 1994-95 respectively due to the improper land management and chemical utilization. Thus, the soil degradation had increased from 160 m.h. to 194.5 m.h. in India during the period from 1985-86 to 1994-95.

While out of 46.8 per cent of net area sown during 1994-95, lands under cultivable waste have been steadly declining from 5.1 per cent in 1985-86 to 4.7 per cent in 1994-95.

Regarding the value of the yield rate of crops in India during the period from 1985-86 to 1994-95 yield rate of rice, maize had decreased from Rs. 1274 to Rs. 1911, Rs. 2420 to Rs. 1448 respectively during the study period.

In India, the cultivable land area decreased from 16.60 million hecate in 1985-86 to 14.26 million hectare in 1994-95. Despite, there was some development in Government project in Tamil Nadu from 1985-86 to 1994-95, the cultivable land had decreased from 32.20 m.h. to 29.07 m.n. The variation in the cultivable land in various year depends upon the steepness slopes, ruggedness of terrain, soil fertility, among of soil and wind erosion.

In India, the cropping intensity had raised from 126.55 million hectare to 131.50 million hectare during the study period. Besides, there was hardly and difference in intensity of cropping in irrigated any unirrigated areas. The cropping intensity of agriculture was low as compare to that in similar condition in other countries.

The area under current fallow land had decreased from 14.81 million hectare to 13.25 million hectare during study period. It is found that 0.6 percentage of current fallow land decreased due to the vagaries of monsoon which might to keep their lands fallow.

It is estimated that the production of total foodgrains increased at the rate of 6 per cent and that rice and pulses at the rate of 10 per cent and 20 per cent respectively in the sub region. The growth rate of foodgrains production varied depend upon the level of irrigation, use of agricultural inputs and prevailing climate condition during the reported agricultural season.

The net area under irrigation had increased from 41.86 m.h.a. in 1985-86 to 53.00 m.h.a in 1994-95.The development of irrigation potential is largely due to the efforts of the Government in the development of irrigation facilities through major, medium and minor irrigation projects.

Ground water sources contributed nearly 51 per cent of the total area irrigated in 1991-92. These has been a drastic increase in the utilistion of ground water resources, rivers, canals, tanks have also been affected considerably due to the degradation and dilatation of riverbeds.

The total water requirements of crops varies from 10.6 acre inches for mustard to 95.0 acre-inches for sugarcane. The water needs of other crops are what 14.8; maize 17.8 bajwar 25.7 groundnut 26.1, ragi 29.8 chillies 28.8, tobacco 29.2, rice 41.7 and cotton 42.2 acre inches.

In addition to the crops, the water requirements of delicious fruit trees is about 30 inches, and of citrus and evergreen tree about 40 inches a year. Touch crops such as beans, lettuce and water melons require about 16 inches of water, common feeder grasses about 24 inches and perennial legumes such as lucerne, berseen and clover about 36 inches of water per year. When the required quantity is not available through natural water supply, irrigation has to be resorted to.

India's total geographical area of 328 m. hectares lies in topical and subtropical zones. The total cultivable areas is 256 m. hectares, and the net sown are was 138m. hectares and the gross cropped areas(including area cropped more than once) was 164 m. hectares.

The total land area in the country under food crops is 118 m. hectares. There are 52.60 m. hectares in the Indo-Gangetic plain (i.e. six states of Punjab, Haryana, Rajasthan, Uttar Pradesh, Bihar and West Bengal). In Central India (i.e. Gujarat, Madhya Pradesh, Maharashtra and Orissa) the sown areas for food grains is 38.4 m hectares; while in peninsular India (Kerala, Karnataka, Andhra Pradesh and Tamil Nadu) the food crops are grown on 22.6 hectares. The productivity differ considerably from zone and from state to state. While in Punjab and Tamil Nadu a hectare yield of food production entirely depends on the difference in availability of water for the land either through rain or artificial supplies.

The consumption of fertilizers had increased from 21.8 lakhs tonnes in 1970-71 to about 91 lakh tones in 1987-88 consumption of phosphetic and potassic fertilizers are increasing in the past green revolution periods.

The Nitrogen uses are higher than the (36.8 lakhs tonnes) phosphate and potassic (12.1 lakhs tonnes and 6.2 lakhs tonnes) in 1985-86. It implies that the total Nitrogen, Phospatic, Potassic uses are increased from 55.2 lakhs tonnes to 115.1 lakhs tonnes during the study period.

The number of population below poverty line in 1999-2000 among other states, Tamil Nadu is in the top most list i.e. 20.55 per cent of person in rural and 22.11 per cent of person in urban areas.

The yield of rice crops was 2372 Kgs per hectare in 1985-86 and it has increased to 2392 Kgs per hectare in 1994-95. The changes in the yield of other crops are: cholam from 1057 to 1134 kgs per hectare, cumbu from 1915 kgs to 1708 kgs per hectare. Ragi from 1542 kgs to 1953 kgs per hectare, maize from 473 kgs to 492 kgs per hectare. But the yield of maize decreased from 1858 kgs per hectre to 1522 kgs hectare and the millets also declined from 615 kgs hectare to 564 kgs per hectare during the period from 1985-86 to 1995-96.

It is estimated that the reduction in the cropped area was 0.35 lakhs hectares for rice crops,3 lakhs hectares for cholam crops, 0.85 lakhs hectred for cumbu, 0.26 lakhs hectares for ragi, 0.49 lakhs hectare for maize and 0.15 lakhs hectare for other millets crops, but area under cultivation of total pulses had increased 1.09 lakhs during the study period.

In 1985-86, of the total reporting area of 130.0 lakhs hectares, 11.82 lakhs hectare was current fallow land which denotes 9.09 per cent of the Tamil Nadu state.

Of the total geographical area (130 1.ha), 64.8 1.ha (50 per cent) was under cropped area in 1985-86, it had increased to 70.3 lakhs hectares (54 per cent) in 1994-95. Though rice stands as the first crop, it covered less than one third of food cropped area in the sub-region and nearly one-half of the state.

During 1985-86, intensity of cultivation in Tamil Nadu was worked out to 121.4 lakhs hectare against 121.6 lakhs hectare in 1994-95. The higher degree of intensity of cultivation in Tamil Nadu may be attributed to light position of cultivated land which also reflected and increase the intensity of cropping cultivation by 0.2 lakhs hectare during the study periods.

The percentage of area irrigated by canal had come down from 42 per cent in 1950-51 to 29.07 per cent in 1994-95. However there is undulating trend in case of area irrigated by tanks. The total net area irrigated had shown an upward trend from 18.55 l.h.a. to 29.03 1.h.a.

The net area sown had increased from 93568 hectare in 1985-86 to 107808 hecatare in 1994-95 and similarly the uncultivable land had increased from 4310 hectare to 4317 hectare during the same period.

The cultivable waste land had increased from 5321 hectare to 6878 hectare during the study period. The cultivable waste land increased year by year and accumulated the land pollution.

The fallow land has increased from 29515 hectare in 1985-86 to 48771 hectare in 1994-95, due to the dumping of wastages in the land.

The area of paddy crop had decreased from 159293 hectare in 1985-86 to 28905 hectare in 1994-95 and the area of gingelly had increased from 3978 hectare in 1985-86 to 4332 in 1994-95. Of the total irrigated area, only 40 per cent of lands irrigated by tanks.

The soil of Sattur, Srivilliputtur and Arupukottai is black loams which is suited for the cultivation of cotton, chillies and millets. The red soil of munnur, Watrap and Natampatti area of Srivilliputtur taluk and Triruchuly Taluk is highly suited for groundnut, gingelly, and onion in Virudunagar District.

Of the total forest area of 1,24,321 ha, farm forestry plantations covered 9,158 ha, and 2,150 ha. of economic plantations. The quick growing plantations had raised to the extent of 1,361 during the period from 1985-86 to 1994-95 in Tirunelveli district.

In Tirunelveli District, waste and fallow lands had extended to the level of 70,000 ha. These waste and fallow lands are increasing by every year. Of the total area of 40954 hectare, 185048 hectare (42 per cent) are brought under the cultivation of different crops.

The uncultivable waste land had increased from 68,910 hectare to 70159 hectare during period from 1985-86 to 1994-95 i.e. increase of 1249 hectare of uncultivable waste land during the period of Turicorin district.

The study found that current fallow land had decreased from 45214 hecatare to 40884 hectare and cropped area had increased from 219381 hectare to 222471 hectare in 1985-86 to 1994-95 in Tuticorin district and thereby raising the cropped area to 3099 hectares.

The study found that average land owned by the small farmers was 2.0 acres Rs 27230 of land and 1.94 acres of wet land Rs 52845. The average land area owned by the marginal farmers was 3.47 acre of wet land (Rs. 52843) and 3.1 acres of dry lands Rs. 48667. The average land owned by the large farmers was 6.10 acres of wet land Rs. 110116 and 6.32 acres of dry land Rs 167305 in the year 2001-02.

The study reveals that changes in the annual income of the respondents was Rs. 310327.4 for small farmers,

Rs 65466.3 for marginal farmers and Rs 11,131.2 for large farmers during the period from 1993-94 and 2001-02. It was found that annual income of marginal farmers was less than the small and large farmers annual income due to the inefficiency and low utilization of input with higher cost capital in the land.

The average annual household savings of the small, marginal and large farmer was Rs. 528.7, Rs. 1019.9 and Rs. 1937 respectively in 1993-94, while compared in 2001-02, the average annual household savings of the small, marginal and large farmer was Rs. 440, Rs. 969 and Rs. 1601 respectively. The savings level have been declined drawing the study period.

The average cultivated area with own land was 17,708 acre in Aruppukottai block, 19.366 acre in Tenkasi and 20.488 acre in Srivilliputtur block in 1993-94 and it has decreased to 16.318 acre in Aruppukotai block. 17.167 acres in Tenkasi block and 18.468 acre in Srivaikundam block in 2001-02. It shows that there is reduction in the average cultivated area in the study districts.

The average land irrigated was 13.594 acre in Aruppukottai block in the year 1993-94 and it had decreased to 13.157 acre in 2001-02. It is clear that the average yield per acre on paddy, gingelly, groundnut, cotton, sugar, chillies and plantain was 2475 kg,1280 kg,1690 kg, 1310 kg, 4.00 T.Kilograms, 360 kg., and 650 Tar in 1993-94 and the same figure have decreased to 2220 kg, 1170 kg, 1216 kg, 645 kg., 3.45T., 345 kgs 600 Tar in 2001-02.

In these three blocks, the changes in paddy crop yield per acre shows the declining trend to the extent of 370 kgs in Aruppukottai block, 615 kgs. in Tenkasi block and 255 kgs in Srivaikundam block during the study periods.

The changes during the period of 1993-94 and 2001-02 in the average use of quantity of pesticide on paddy, groundnut pulses, gingelly, ragi, sugar, plantain, vegetables, and chillies was 0.45 litre, 0.4 litre, 0.3 litre, .57 litre, .4 litre,

0.8 litre, 1 litre, 0.3 litre and 0.4 litre at the value of Rs. 415, Rs. 260, Rs. 1160, Rs. 610, Rs. 450, Rs. 260, Rs. 750, Rs. 1120, and Rs. 585 respectively

Regarding the opinion of the respondents, the 45.29 per cent of respondents accepted efforts on water resource management, 33.96 per cent of respondent favoured the efforts to change of cultivation. The 20.75 per cent of respondents suggested for soil erosion control and control for the use of chemical fertilizer in the land are the suitable measures of the protection from environment degradation and enhancing economic status of the farmers.

SUGGESTIONS

The main suggestions of the study are

1. The suggestion can also be upgraded technology. It can be started with use of manual land animal power and upgraded to the use of small-scale, simple machinery. As in most places throughout the world, a rudimentary tradition of exploiting groundwater exists and therefore, development of groundwater resources should start with the use of indigenous technologies. More than any other water resources, groundwater has higher level of safety from the public wealth point of views.

2. Since the power for energisation of wells is free, it induced the farmers to dig more number of wells. As a result of this, many ground water structures in some areas have become dry. So it is necessary that artificial recharge schemcs have to be taken up to induce recharge wherever there is heavy depletion of groundwater level.

3. Presently power is supplied at free of cost to farmers for agricultural pump sets. Since power is made available free, there may be haphazard way of pumping over and above the actual irrigation requirements. So, regarding the depleting the groundwater storage, some kind of reconsideration

is necessary for supply of power at free of cost to farmers. Small and marginal farmers may be supplied free power, whereas power should not be supplied at free of cost to big farmers. If power is given at free of cost, that may encourage the farmers to sink more well and thereby there will be heavy extraction and depletion of groundwater level.

4. The agricultural development can be steady while one can adopt suitable cropping patterns which consume less water wherever there is scarcity of water.

5. Water conservation should be treated as starting and central point in watershed management. Watershed management should become people's movement and governments, donor and other funding agencies, NGOs etc. should participate in the people's program by providing, technical advice and social stimulate.

6. Conservation measures should be considered as a means and production systems as an end.

7. Holistic and mixed farming systems should be promoted and role of livestock should be appreciated.

8. Low cost, simple and vegetative conservation technology based on indigenous technical know should be promoted with water shed community's initiative and with minimum external support.

9. Water shed approach, soil erosion, policy measures to arrest soil erosion, making water development process functional, judicious irrigation, Gypsum application, Organic manuring, Balanced fertilization, Desertification, Integrated need management including use of bio-fertilizers, Desertification, Integrated need management including use of bio-fertilizers, organic manures, Vermicompost, Agrochemical registration,

Agrochemical restriction on use, proper soil weather including monitor changes in soil properties, proper cropmix and crop rotations are some of the important suggestions of the study to protect the environment degradation and reduce the rural poverty in backward regions of Tamil Nadu.

CONCLUSION

Till recently, many efforts were directed at assessing and monitoring soil degradation in India, while opened new vistas to assess soil degradation with sufficient reliability. This can serve as a base for monitoring regional level changes in soil degradation using remotely sensed data and GIS technology. The study conclude that unless short and long term measures are taken to assess our basic soil resources in order to arrest degradation and restore productivity, we may not be ale to fulfill our obligation towards pasturing, who may otherwise ask the question. "Here is the land but where is the soil".

BIBLIOGRAPHY

BOOKS

Abbasai, S.A. *"Environmental Impact Assessment"*, Discovery Publishing House, New Delhi, 2000.

Abbasi, S.A. and F.I. Khan, *"Green Belts for Pollution Abatement"* Discovery Publishing House, New Delhi, 2000.

Anil Kumar and Pandey, R.N, *"Wasteland Management In India"*, Ashish Publishing House, New Delhi, 1989.

Ballara Marcela, *"Women and Literacy"*, Non-Governmental Iason Service, Geneva, 1991.

Bardhan, P.K *"Land, Labour, and Rural Poverty"*, Oxford University Press, Delhi, 1984.

Bartelmus, P. Lutz, and Tongern J.V., *"Environmental Operational Perspective"* in Serogeldin, I and Steer, A., (eds) "Valuing the Environment Environmentally Sustainable Development Proceeding Series", The World Bank, Washington, 1994.

Bella Abzug, *"Social Priorities of Civil Society"*, Non-Governmental Liaison Service, Geneva, 1995.

Bhattacharya, N. and *et al.*, *"Poverty Inequality and Prices in Rural India"*, Sage Publication India Pvt. Ltd. New Delhi, 1991.

Blaikie, Piers, *"The Political Economy of Soil Erosion in Developing Countries"*, Longman, Londan and New York, 1998.

Brand C. and K. Hommann, *"The Cost of Inaction:Valuing the Economy-Wide cost of Environmental Degradation in India"*, Mimeo Asia Environment Division, World Bank, 1995.

Chambers, Robert, N.C. Saxena and Tushaar Shah. *To the Hands of the Poor Water and Trees.* Oxford & IBH. Publishing Co. New Delhi, 1989.

Chen, Shaohua and Martin Ravailion, *"How Did the World's Poorest Fare in the 1990's"?* Research Working Paper. World Bank, Washington, December, 2000.

Dandekar, V.M. *"The Indian Economy, 1947-92 Vol. II: Population, Poverty and Employment*, Sage Publications India Pvt. Ltd. New Delhi, 1996.

Deepa Narayan and Others, *"Voices of the Poor: Crying Out for Change"*, Oxford University Press, World Bank, New York, 2000.

Dhawan, B.D, *"Inter-source Differences in Productivity of Irrigated Agriculture."* In B.D. Dhawan, (ed.,) Irrigation in India's Agricultural Development: Productivity, Stability, Equity, Sage Publications, New Delhi, 1989, pp. 114-33.

Dhawan, B.D. *"Studies in Minor Irrigation With Special Reference to Ground Water"*, Commonwealth Publishers, New Delhi, 1990.

Joshi, P.K. and N.K. Jyagi, *"Soil Affected and Waterlossed Soils in India"*, in M. Avendson and A. Gulati (Eds) Stategic Changes in Indian Irrigation, Mac Millian India Ltd., Delhi, 1995.

Kakwani, N.C. *"Income Inequality and Poverty"*, Oxford University Press, New York 1980.

Kanchan Chopra, S.C. Gulati, *"Migration, Common Property Resources And Environment Degradation"* Sage Publications. New Delhi, 2001, Rs. 295/-

Kausik, K.K. *"Sustainable Agriculture: Issues and Policy Implications"* in K.C. Roy, H.C. Blomquist and I. Hossain (Eds) Development That Lasts, New Age International Publishers, New Delhi, 1997.

Khoshoo, T.N. and B.L, Deekshatulu, *"Land and Soils"*, Indian National Science Academy, Har-Anand Publications, New Delhi, 1992.

Lewis Owen and Tim Unwin, *"Environmental Management-Reading and Case Studies"*, Blackwell Publishers Ltd. Oxford, United Kingdom, 1997.

Malcom Hadly (ed), *"EcoSystem Rehabilitation of the Rural landscape in South and Central Asia: An Analysis of Issues,* "Regional Office of Science and Technology for South and Central, Asia, New Delhi, 1994.

Mathur, O.P., *"Public Expenditure on Water"*, National Institute of Public Finance Policy, New Delhi, 1998.

Murthy J.V.S., *"Watershed Management in India"*, Wiley Eastern Limited, Chennai, 1994.

Nandkarni M.V. *"Agriculture and Environment"* in M.S. Rathore (Ed), Environment and Development, Rawat Publications, Jaipur, 1996.

Narayan, Deepa, with Raj Patel, Kai Sohaffi, Anne Rademacher, and Sarah Koch Schulte, *"Can Anyone Hear Us? Voices of the Poor"*, Oxford University Press, New York, 2000.

Palanisamy, K. and K.W. Easter, *"Tank Irrigation in the 21st Century: What Next?"*, Discovery Publishing House, New Delhi, 2000.

Quentin T. Wodon, *"Poverty and Policy in Latin America and the Corribbean*, World Bank, Technical Paper, No 467, Washington, 2000.

Ramakrishnan, P.S, U.M. Chandrashekara and etal, *"Mountain Biodiversity, Land Use Dynamics, and Traditional Ecological Knowledge"*, Oxford & IBH Publishing Co. Pvt. Ltd, New Delhi, 2000.

Ramakrishnan, R.S. Shifting Agriculture and Sustainable Development of North, Eastern India USESCO-MAB series, Paris, Oxford University Press, New Delhi, 1993.

Ramakrishnan. P.S. and *et al.*, (ed), *"Himalayen Environment and Sustainable Development*, Diamond Jublee Publications, New Delhi, 1994.

Ramkrishnan, P.S. and *et al.*, *"Conserving the Sacred for Biodiversity Management"*, Oxford and IBH Publishng Co. Pvt. Ltd., New Delhi.

Repetto, R., "The *"Second India"* Revisited ;Population, Poverty and Environmental Stress Over Two Decades", World Resource Institute, Washington, December, 1994.

Rodda Annabal, *"Women and the Environment"*, Non-Governmental Liaison Service, Geneva, 1991.

Roger Jaffery, A and Nandini Sundar, *"A New Moral Economy for India's Forests?"*, Sage Publications, New Delhi, 1999.

Sanker U, and Mathur, O.P.(eds), *"Economics Instruments for Environment Sustainability"*, National Insurance of Public Finance and Policy and Madras School of Economics, 1998.

Sanker, U. "On the Allocation of Joint and Common Costs", in N.S.S. Narayana and A. Sen (eds) *"Poverty. Environment and Economic Development"*, Interline, Bangalore, 1994.

Srinivasan T.N. "International Trade and the Environment N.S.S. Narayana and A.Sen (eds), *Poverty, Environment and Economic Development*, Interline, Bangalore, 1995.

Walker, B. and Steffer, W. (Ed), *"The Terrestrial Biosphere and Global Change: Implications for Natural and Management Eco System-A Synthesis of GCTE and Related Research* 'IGBP' Sweden, 1997.

World Bank, *'India Irrigation Sector Review, Agriculture and Water Division*, Washington, South Asia, December 2, 1991.

JOURNALS

Abluwalia, M.S. *"Rural Poverty and Agricultural Performance in India"*, Journal of Development Studies, Vol. 14, No. 3, April, 1978.

Anju Sharma and Meenu Sood, "Women Land and Forests", *Kisan World* February, 1997.

Arul Qnana Sekar, "Micro Watersheds and Agriculture A case Study", *Journal of Extension and Research*, Vol. III, No. 1 and 2, January, 2001.

Bardhan, D.K. "On the Incidence of Poverty in Rural India of the Sixties, *Economic and Political Weekly*, Vol.8, Nos 4-6, February, 1973.

Chinniah, R. and A. Thahasahad, "Ground Water Management Problem", Peninsular Economist, Vol. XI, No. 1, 1998-99.

Cropper, M.L. and Oates, W.E,. "Environmental Economics: A Survey, "Journal of Economic Literature, Vol. 30, 1992.

Dandekar, "On Measurement of Poverty", *Economic and Political Weekly*, Vol. 16, No 30. July 25, 1981.

Danny M. Leipziger, "The Unfinished Poverty Agenda: Why Latin American and the Caribbean hag Behind", *Finance and Development*, Vol. 38, No 1, March, 2001.

David Pugh, "Sea Level Change: Meeting the Challenge", *Natural Resources*, Vol. 33, No. 3-4, 1997, pp. 26-32.

Editorials, "Concern over Environmental Degradation", *The Hindu*, November 15, 2000.

Editorials, "Forest Department Project helps create awareness on biodiversity Conservation", *The Hindu*, December 10, 2000.

Editorials, "Good Response to Green Belt Project", *The Hindu*, November 28, 2000.

Ganesamoorthy, "Sustainable Development and Environment Role in Land" *Peninsular Economist*, Vol. XI, No 1, 1998-99.

Ghosh, D.K, "NGO Intervention in Poverty Alleviation: Scope and Reality" *Kurukshetra*, Vol. 49, No 5, March, 2001.

Gilbert Etimenne, "Eradicating Rural Poverty", *The Hindu*, November 21, 2000.

Gouranga Kar, "Remote Sensing for Instainable Watershed Management", *Kurukshetra*, Vol. 49, No 6, March, 2001.

Hanumantha Rao C.H., "Liberalisation of Agriculture in India, some Major Issues", *Indian Journal of Agricultural Economics*, Vol. 3, July-September, 1995.

Jagannath Pati, "Women, Environment and Sustainable Rural Development", *Kurukshetra*, Vol. 48. No. 12, September, 2000.

Janakarajan "Consequence of Aquifer over exploitation", *Review of Development and Change*, Vol. II, No 1, Jan-June, 1997.

Jean Drez, "Starving the Poor-I", *The Hindu*, February 26, 2001.

Jules. N. Pretty, *"Regenerating Agriculture Politics and Practice for Sustainability and Self-Reliance"*, Vikas Publishing House Pvt. Ltd., New Delhi, 1996.

Kanchan Chopra, "Sustainability of Agriculture", *Indian Journal of Agriculture Economics,* Vol. 48, No. 3, July-September, 1993.

Kannan K.P. "Declining incidence of Rural Poverty in Kerala", *Economic and Political Weekly*, Vol. 30, No 41 & 42, October 14-21, 1995.

Karhikeyan C and N. Rajamohan, "Economic Utilisation and Conservation of Rural Environmental Resources", *Peninsular Economist*, Vol. XI, No. 1, 1998-99.

Kasthurbai Thanasekaran, "Agricultural Technology and Sustainable Development", *Peninsular Economist*, Vol. XI, No 1, 1998-99.

Lal, S. and A.K. Singh, "How to Sustain Agriculture", *Indian Farming*, April, 1997.

Marothia D.K, "Agriculture Technology and Environmental Quality", Indian Journal of *Agricultural Economics*, Vol. 52, No. 3, July-September, 1997.

Murugan, S.V. "Sustainable Agriculture Importance in the context of Environmental Degradation and Population Explosion: *Peninsular Economist*, Vol. XI, No. 1, 1998.

Muthu Raja, C. "Rural Women in Indian Agriculture *'Khadi Gramodyog*, Vol. 36, No. 8, 1990.

Muthu Raja,C. "Poverty Eradication in India", Poverty *Eradication Foundation Bulletin*, Vol. 1, No 1. July-September, 1991.

Muthukumar P.K. and Rajendran, "Voluntary Organisation and Sustainable Development of Water Resources", *Peninsular Economist*, Vol. XI, No. 1, 1998-90.

Nadkarni, M.V. "Acceleration of Commercialisation of Agriculture, Dynamic Agriculture and Stagnatic Peasants", *Economic and Political Weekly*, June 29, 1996.

Nair, M.D. "WTO Agreement on Agriculture: Strategic Issues for India", *The Hindu*, December 14, 2000.

Neek Mukherjee, "Migration Women from West Bengal III-Being and Well-Being", *Economic and Political Weekly*, Vol. XXXVI, No. 26, June 30, 2001.

Nikkantha Rath, *"Agricultural Growth and Investment in India"* Journal of the Indian School of Political Economy. Vol. 1, No I, Jan-June, 1989.

Parthasarathy, G "Public Intervention and Rural Poverty: Case of Non-Sustainable Reduction Andhra Pradesh; *Economic and Political Weekly*, Vol. 30, Nos. 41-42. October 14-21, 1995.

Prakash, R. and K. Thanunathan. "Growing Traditional Rice Varieties: Boon for Sustainable Development in Rice Farming under low Input Management", *Peninsular Economist*, Vol. XI, No. 1, 1998-99.

Rajeer, M.S. and *et. al.*, "Crop sequence with Retoon Rice: A way for Sustainable Agriculture in Flood Prone Areas", *Peninsular Economist*, Vol. XI, No. 1, 1998-99.

Rammanohar Reddy, C "Agriculture's Plight", *The Hindu*, December 23, 2000.

Rammanohar Reddy, C. "Poverty and Employment in the 1990's", *The Hindu*, January 20, 2001.

Rammanohar Reddy. C, "Watershed Development: Eco Power", *The Hindu Survey of Environment*, 1997.

Robert, G. Wild and Jackson Mutebi," Bwindi Impenetrable Forest, Vganda: Conservation through Collaborative Management, *Natural Resources.* Vol. 33, No. 3-4, 1997, pp. 33-51.

Roy, B.K. 1991, "Water availability in India", *Water Resources Development*, Vol. 7, No. 2, June, 1991.

Sankaram Ayala, "Eco-Technology Focus for Sustainability in Farming" *The Hindu*, December 7, 2001.

Sen, Abhijit, "Rural Labour Market and Poverty", *Indian Journal of Labour Economics*, Vol. 37, No 4, October-December, 1994.

Seth, S.L. "Watershed Management in India", Kurukshetra. Vol. 48,No 9, June, 2000, pp. 2-7.

Shete, N.B. "Sustainable Rural and Agricultural Development: Some Views', *Indian Economic Ponorama*, December, 1995.

Shrivastava, M.M.P., "Sustainable Development with Special Reference to Environment and Agriculture", *Journal of Rural Development*, Vol. 13, No. 1, 1994.

Shylendra, H.S. "Institutional Reform and Rural Poor: A study on the distributional performance of a Rural Bank", *Indian Journal of Agricultural Economics*, Vol. 51, No 3, July-September, 1996.

Susan M. Braatz, "State of the World's Forest, 1997, Natural Resources, Vol. 33, No. 3-4, 1997, pp. 18-25.

Swaminathan M.S., "Ecological Farming", Survey of India-Agriculture, *The Hindu*, Madras, 1994.

Swaminathan, M.S. "Shaping our Agriculture Future", *The Hindu*, January 11, 2001.

Thandavakumari, K. "Sustainable Development and Environment Management through Integrated Watershed Programme", *Peninsular Economist*, Vol. XI, No. 1, 1998-99.

Tyagi, D.S. "How Valid are the Estimates of Trends in Rural Poverty?, *Economic and Political Weekly*, Vol. 17, No 26, June, 1982.

Vandana Shiva. "Agriculture Policy, Budget and WTO", *The Hindu*, March 6, 2001.

Venkatesh, V. "Experiments with Poverty in Andhra Pradesh and Rajasthan", The Hindu, December 12, 2000.

Vohra B.B, "Agenda for Water: Myth and Reality", Survey of the Environment. *The Hindu*, Madras, 1994.

Vyapuri, V.P. *et. al.*, "Economically Viable Agronomic Practices Towards Sustainability in Rice-Block Gram Cropping System for Cavery Delta", *Peninsular Economist*, Vol. XI, No. 1, 1998-99.

Wang Qinghue, "Forest Management and Terroved Agriculture: Case study of hani of Ailao mountains, yunnan" *Economic and Political Weekly*, Vol. XXXVI, No 30, August 3, 2001.

Yu Xiaogeng, "Conflict in Resource Management for Ecosystem Services", Water in Lashi Watershed, lijiang, *Economic and Political Weekly*, Vol. XXXVI, No 30, August 3, 2000.

Yyas, V.S. and Pradeep Bhargva, "Public Intervention for Poverty Alleviation: An Overview *"Economic and Political Weekly,"* Vol. 30, Nos. 41-41, October 14-21, 1995.

REPORTS

Government of India, *"Status of Ground Water Pollution in India"*, Faridabad: Ground Water Pollution Directorate, Central Ground Water Board, Ministry of Water Resources, 1991.

Government of India, *"Report of the Ninth Plan Working Group on Major and Medium Irrigation Programmes"*, Planning Commission, New Delhi, 1996.

Government of India, *"Report of the Sub-Committee on Irrigation for the India Water Resources Sector Review"*, Central Water Commission, Ministry of Water Resources, New Delhi, 1997.

Government of India, *"Report of the Committee on Pricing of Irrigation Water"*, Planning Commission, New Delhi, 1992.

Thandavakumari K., *"Watershed and Wasteland Development Technology Field Work and Placement at Scope"*, A Unpublished Study Report Submitted to the Centre for Adult, Continuing Education and Extension, 1996.

INDEX